I'm on Facebook —Now What??? (2nd Edition)

How To Use Facebook To Achieve Business Objectives

**By Jason Alba,
Jesse Stay, and Rachel Melia**
Foreword by Mari Smith
Afterword by Michael Stelzner

20660 Stevens Creek Blvd., Suite 210
Cupertino, CA 95014

Published by Happy About®
20660 Stevens Creek Blvd., Suite 210, Cupertino, CA 95014
http://happyabout.com

2nd Edition: March 2013
1st Edition: January 2008
Paperback ISBN (2nd Edition): 978-1-60005-232-3 (1-60005-232-0)
Paperback ISBN (1st Edition): 978-1-60005-095-4 (1-60005-095-6)
eBook ISBN (2nd Edition): 978-1-60005-233-0 (1-60005-233-9)
eBook ISBN (1st Edition): 978-1-60005-096-1 (1-60005-096-4)
Place of Publication: Silicon Valley, California, USA
Paperback Library of Congress Number: 2008921423

A Message from Happy About®

Thank you for your purchase of this Happy About book. It is available online at http://happyabout.com/facebook.php or at other online and physical bookstores.

- Please contact us for quantity discounts at sales@happyabout.info
- If you want to be informed by email of upcoming Happy About® books, please email bookupdate@happyabout.info

Happy About is interested in you if you are an author who would like to submit a non-fiction book proposal or a corporation that would like to have a book written for you. Please contact us by email editorial@happyabout.info or phone (1-408-257-3000).

Other Happy About books available include:

- I'm on LinkedIn—Now What???(3rd Edition):
  http://www.happyabout.com/linkedinhelp.php
- I'm at a Networking Event—Now What???.
  http://www.happyabout.com/networking-event.php
- I've Got a Domain Name—Now What???:
  http://www.happyabout.com/ivegotadomainname.php
- I'm in a Job Search—Now What???:
  http://www.happyabout.com/jobsearchnowwhat.php
- Internet Your Way to a New Job:
  http://www.happyabout.com/InternetYourWaytoaNewJob.php
- Storytelling about Your Brand Online & Offline:
  http://www.happyabout.com/storytelling.php
- Social Media Success!:
  http://www.happyabout.com/social-media-success.php
- #SOCIAL MEDIA PR tweet Book01:
  http://www.thinkaha.com/social-media-pr-tweet-book01/
- #GOOGLE+ for BUSINESS tweet Book01:
  http://www.thinkaha.com/google-plus-for-business-tweet01/
- 42 Rules of Social Media for Small Business:
  http://www.happyabout.com/42rules/social-media-business.php
- 42 Rules for B2B Social Media Marketing:
  http://happyabout.com/42rules/b2bsocialmediamarketing.php
- 42 Rules for a Web Presence that Wins:
  http://www.happyabout.com/42rules/winningwebpresence.php
- The Digital and Direct Marketing Goose
  http://www.happyabout.com/digitalgoose.php

C o n t e n t s

Foreword By Mari Smith

We are living in a "relationship economy" like never before. Yes, technology has evolved rapidly over the past decade, but then, so has our collective consciousness and our desire to connect with our fellow humans...and to share more openly with one another.

So, it seems the vision of Mark Zuckerberg—CEO and cofounder of Facebook—**to make the world more open and connected**, is actually coming to fruition and we are all willing helpers. This is a very good thing.

While it's always been true that people do business with people they know, like, and trust, the explosion of online social networking has led us to experience a fundamental paradigm shift in how we communicate—and ultimately, do business—on a global basis.

Facebook, the world's largest social networking site, is at the center of this explosion. To take advantage of this new paradigm, it is critical that businesses and organizations of all sizes understand how to best utilize it.

We have to keep in mind, though, that every social network has a unique culture...and Facebook is certainly no exception. It's important to understand that hundreds of millions of daily active users are on the platform multiple times a day primarily to connect with their friends. Business-related messages are seen as intrusive.

There's a fine art to nurturing relationships with customers and prospects when they are in the midst of social activities.

In fact, Facebook's culture is particularly unique insofar as much of the platform is still very much a "walled garden." (Unlike a site like Twitter, for example, where—unless a user chooses to protect their tweets—then all content is public, save for direct private messages).

Users do have tremendous granular control over who sees what content. (The pushback we see in the media about privacy issues on Facebook so often stems from insufficient education about exactly how to properly use these privacy controls.)

Plus, from a commercial standpoint, Facebook offers businesses of all sizes an array of tools and features to reach a highly-targeted audience. Not only to reach these audiences, but to foster deep engagement, to respond promptly, to enhance customer service, and deliver tremendous value.

Prior to when we had access to such open forms of communicating with our prospects and customers, most all of this engagement would be conducted behind the scenes via phone and email, one person at a time. Now, as a well-respected business or brand, you get to demonstrate your customer relationship skills and impact your reputation and brand sentiment right out in the open for all the public to see. We're being called to higher standards of ethics, transparency, and good business practices. And, when Facebook users get a favorable response to their posts and comments, they are much more likely to make a buying decision. This, too, is a very good thing.

Those that master building and nurturing relationships on Facebook are gaining market share, influence, and increasing sales. And with Facebook's continuing growth in popularity, already well past the 1 billion user mark, Facebook will become even more important for successful commerce in the coming months and years.

As anyone who knows me can attest, I am passionate about Facebook and the opportunities it offers everyone from solopreneurs to household name brands. Effective use of Facebook has been key to my success and I continue to see the positive impact that it has made with my clients, students, and audiences all over the world year after year.

I truly hope you too can benefit from marketing on the Facebook platform!

Cheers,
Mari

Mari Smith
Social Media Thought Leader
Co-author, *Facebook Marketing: An Hour a Day* (2010 and 2012)
Author, *The New Relationship Marketing* (2011)
http://marismith.com
http://facebook.com/marismith
@marismith

Introduction

Jason Alba wrote *I'm on LinkedIn—Now What???* in 2007 to help business professionals understand the power of LinkedIn and how to best utilize the property for career benefit. Rather than being a complicated manual or technology guide, the book was written in easy to understand practical terms.

With the growing popularity of Facebook, Jason recognized the need for a similar book on that topic. In 2008, Jason and Facebook expert Jesse Stay published *I'm on Facebook—Now What???* The book focused on helping people figure out how to derive personal, career, and business benefits from Facebook.

Fast forward five years and Facebook has become the most used social networking platform of all time and a very valuable business marketing tool.

In this updated edition of the book, Facebook Consultant Rachel Melia joins Jason and Jesse to teach organizations of all sizes, from start-ups and small businesses to large organizations, as well as non-profit and government organizations, everything they need to know to be successful on Facebook. We will bring you up to speed on the changes to Facebook since the last edition of this book was published, how to get started with a Facebook Page, how to create engaging content that meets business objectives, how to manage your Facebook Page and build community, how to create successful

Facebook ad buys and promotions, how to measure success, and how to use Facebook applications and plugins.

The book is written in easy to understand language and includes many examples of how successful organizations are using Facebook, as well as Action Items to help you utilize what you learn. We have found that it is really helpful for organizations to have step-by-step instructions and concrete examples so we have also provided those. Since Facebook makes changes rapidly, we risk that the instructions and examples will become inaccurate or outdated, but we think the benefit outweighs the risk. So if you come upon an instruction that has changed, we hope the instructions are close enough that you can find the right way to proceed. We will also share important changes on our Facebook Page https://www.facebook.com/fbbook. We have really enjoyed writing *I'm on Facebook—Now What???* and hope it is a valuable tool in your marketing arsenal. Here's to your Facebook business success!

Jason Alba, CEO
http://www.jibberjobber.com

Jesse Stay, Social Strategist
http://www.jessestay.com/

Rachel Melia, Facebook Consultant
http://rachelmelia.com/

1 What's New Since The Last Edition

Five years is a long time in the world of the internet and social media. Over that time, Facebook has experienced major changes in terms of growth as well as changes to the product.

Growth

The first edition of this book, published in 2008, compared the up-and-coming Facebook to the behemoth at that time, MySpace. At the time, Facebook had 70 million users compared to MySpace's 200 million registered users.

How times have changed. Facebook has experienced massive growth over the last several years and currently has over 1 billion active users (Facebook). As a comparison, YouTube has over 800 million unique visitors per month (YouTube), Twitter has 500 million accounts and 150 million active users (AllTwitter 3/12), LinkedIn has over 175 million members (LinkedIn), Google+ has 100 million monthly active users (Google 10/12), Instagram has over 80 million registered users (Instagram), and

Pinterest has over 11.7 million members (Go-Gulf.com 5/12). MySpace now has 24 million monthly users (TechCrunch 1/12).

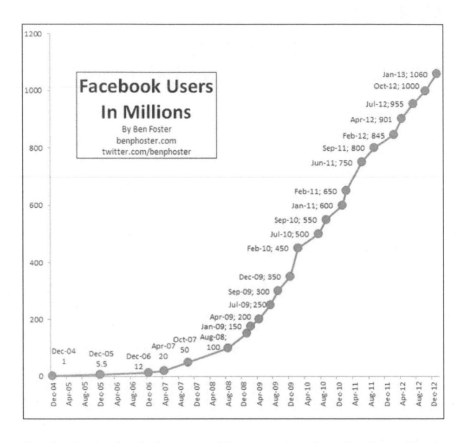

Facebook also leads in terms of time spent on the site. According to Go-Gulf.com (5/12), Facebook and Pinterest are tied for the most time spent on the site per month, at 405 minutes each. The average user spends 89 minutes per month on Twitter, 21 minutes per month on LinkedIn, and 3 minutes per month on Google+.

In addition, Facebook users visit frequently, averaging 58% of users logging in daily (Facebook).

Facebook has also experienced huge growth in mobile usage. More than 50% of Facebook's monthly users, 543 million, access the property using their mobile device each month. Smartphone users visit more frequently, with 50% of smartphone users connecting to Facebook every hour of every day (AllFacebook).

While Facebook was primarily a U.S. site in the early days, it is now used worldwide, with 81% of monthly users outside the U.S. and Canada (Facebook). The following chart shows interesting statistics including number of users by country.

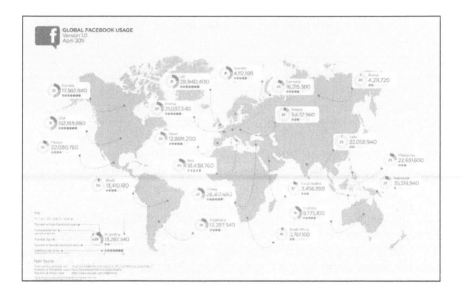

Where there are a large number of users, organizations flock. And organizations have joined Facebook in large numbers. According to a study by Vocus, 73% of small organizations currently use Facebook. According to inSites Consulting, 80% of all U.S. organizations have a Facebook presence.

Product Changes

Beyond the changes in popularity, Facebook has made many changes to the property over the last several years. Facebook makes changes so often it is difficult to keep up. Here are several of the major changes.

Timeline

The most significant major change was the move to Timeline for personal profiles and Pages. Facebook introduced Timeline in September 2011. Mark Zuckerberg called Timeline "the biggest overhaul to the social network since 2008." Timeline is essentially a more visual layout in chronological order. Initially, Timeline was only for personal profiles and users could switch over at their discretion. Facebook introduced Timeline for brands in March 2012. Organizations were forced to switch to Timeline by March 30th 2012, and all personal profiles were switched by July 2012. There was some grumbling at first, but most, especially brands and organizations, like the new layout. We are big fans of Timeline.

With the old Facebook Page format, organizations needed to hire a designer and developer to customize a Page and create unique tabs. Now it is much easier to make the Page visually pleasing yourself.

Timeline includes a large image at the top of the Page and tab images that can be easily switched out. With Timeline, images appear much larger on the Page, and a Page owner can easily Highlight an image (make it much larger on the Page), pin it to the top of the Page, as well as add significant dates to their Timeline. We will dive more into Timeline later.

Other major changes include the announcement of Facebook's Open Graph API, the launch of Social Plugins, and updates to Insights. More recently, Facebook made changes to Admin capabilities.

Open Graph

Facebook announced the Open Graph API in April 2010. Essentially, it is a platform that connects Facebook to other sites on the web. Facebook Connect was the first element of the Open Graph. Launched in 2008, it allowed users to sign into external websites using their

Facebook account. The Open Graph is an extension of this capability and is a set of programming tools that lets sites get information into and out of Facebook.

Social Plugins

With the release of the API came a number of different plugins. The Like Box and Like Button are two very popular Plugins. Other Plugins include Recommendations, Comments, and more. There are currently eleven plugins in all. The complete list can be found at the Facebook Developer Plugin Page **https://developers.facebook.com/docs/plugins/**. We will go into more detail about the various plugins in the Plugins chapter later in this book.

Like Box

Facebook Insights

Updates to Facebook Insights is another important change since the last edition of this book was published. Insights is Facebook's analytics tool. The tool is available for Pages (not personal profiles) and provides a wealth of interesting data. Insights is accessed via the Admin Panel and provides information including Page Likes, reach, engagement, virality, and more. We will go into detail on Facebook Insights in the Measuring Success chapter.

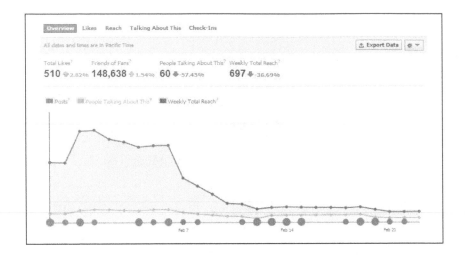

Admin Rights

A recent change to Facebook is the updated admin rights options. In the past, when a person was given admin rights to a Page they had full access to that Page. They could post, view Insights, run an ad buy, and even delete the Page. Having multiple people with full access to a Page made many Page owners nervous.

Facebook has recently rolled out a variety of different roles including Manager, Content Creator, Moderator, Advertiser, and Insights Analyst. A Manager has full admin rights including managing admin roles, sending messages, creating posts as the Page, creating ads, and viewing Insights. A Content Creator can do everything except managing admin roles. A Moderator can respond to posts, an Advertiser can create ad campaigns, and an Insights Analyst can view Insights.

	Manager	Content Creator	Moderator	Advertiser	Insights Analyst
Manage Admin Roles	✓				
Edit the Page and Add Apps	✓	✓			
Create Posts as the Page	✓	✓			
Respond to and Delete Comments	✓	✓	✓		
Send Messages as the Page	✓	✓	✓		
Create Ads	✓	✓	✓	✓	
View Insights	✓	✓	✓	✓	✓

TIP: If you have a Facebook Page and more than one Admin, update the Admin Roles and remove Admin privileges for anyone that is no longer an Admin.

Those are several of the major changes to Facebook since the release of first edition of this book. As mentioned before, Facebook makes changes all the time. Many find it frustrating and difficult to keep up, but Facebook has to be commended for continuing to evolve.

Some other notable changes we will go into in other sections of this book are those to advertising products, the evolution of EdgeRank, the new capability to schedule posts, and the new Facebook Page Manager iPhone application.

ACTION ITEMS

- Look at the Timeline's of a few of your favorite Facebook Pages.

- Go to Insights and check out all the information available.

- Set appropriate Admin Roles and take away Admin privileges for anyone that is no longer an admin.

- To stay up to date on Facebook growth and changes, follow our Facebook Page https://www.facebook.com/fbbook.

2 Getting Started With Facebook

With over 1 billion people on Facebook, we're going to assume most everyone has a personal profile, so we are not going to go into how to set that up. Since Facebook is fairly mature at this point, many organizations are up and running with a business profile, also known as a Facebook Page. For those without a Facebook Page, we're going to walk through setting that up. Those that already have a Facebook Page will also benefit from this section as we will go deeper into customizing your Timeline. We are also going to review how to post and provide suggestions for how to get the word out.

Setting Up A Facebook Page

It's fairly easy to set up a Facebook Page. If you have yet to do that, just follow these steps:

1. Click on "Create a Page" at the bottom of your personal profile or go to this url: **https://www.facebook.com/pages/create.php**. Either way, you will get to this page.

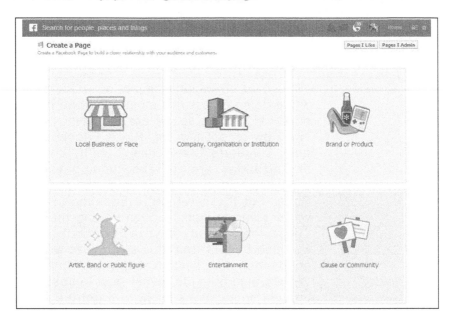

Previously, once you picked a type of Page it could not be changed, but now it can. Pick the one that most represents your type of business, but don't worry too much about this step. You can change the category later, if needed. Hover over the type of Page, then select the category, and add any information requested.

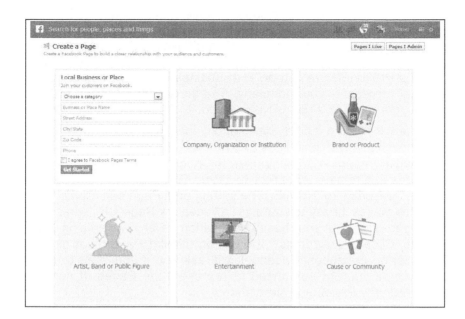

2. Click "Get Started." You will go to a screen where you will be asked to upload a Profile Picture, add About information, and choose your Facebook URL. Depending on the type of Page, you may be asked to provide other information.

3. Now the fun begins. Upload a Profile Picture/thumbnail that is 180x180. If you don't have the exact size, try uploading what you have. A square image is ideal. If your image isn't square you may be able to select an appropriate portion of a non-square image. The Profile Picture can be your business logo or another image that represents your company. The thumbnail will show up next to your posts in a user's News Feed.

4. Then fill in the About information, including basic information about your business, links to your website, and any other social media properties. Next, choose the Facebook URL. In the past a Page had to have 250 Likes to get a URL. That number was then decreased to 25. Now anyone setting up a Page can grab a URL. This makes it easy to share your Facebook Page URL when talking to others, at your business location, in any advertising copy, etc. Click "Set Address." If there are similar Pages that already exist on Facebook, Facebook will ask you if you want to claim them, if you are authorized to represent the Pages. If not, un-check any Pages and click "Skip."

TIP: Information in the "About:" field shows up on your Timeline under the Cover Image. This is a great way to share information about your organization. Consider adding a url as a way to drive traffic back to your website.

---

5. Now you will be routed to your new Page's Admin Panel and Facebook will ask you to Like your Page, Invite Your Friends, and Share Something. Skip if you want to continue perfecting your Page before launching. At this point, you will be on the Page with the Admin Panel open. This is a good time to add your Cover Image. To do this click on "Add a Cover" and upload an 851x315 image. We'll talk more about different types of images you can choose in the next section, Customizing Your Timeline. Your new Page will look something like this.

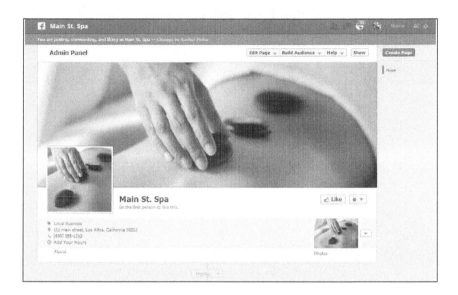

6. Next, you can complete the Page information. To do this click on "Edit Page" and "Update Info."

You will land on this Page and be asked to fill out different information, depending on the type of Page.

Now your basic Facebook Page is set up. Let's talk more about how the Timeline format makes it really easy to customize your Page's look and feel.

Customizing Your Timeline

Facebook calls the Timeline an "empty canvas." Timeline is essentially a blank slate and organizations can easily customize the look and feel as well as functionality of the Page.

Organizations can customize their Timeline with a unique Profile Picture, Cover Image, by adding original Application tab images, and by adding Milestones. Organizations can also add functionality by adding applications (which can be accessed via the tabs). We will go over adding images now and talk about adding applications later, in the Applications chapter.

Here is a handy image that shows where the Profile Picture, Cover Image, and Application Tab Images are on the Timeline, as well as the dimensions.

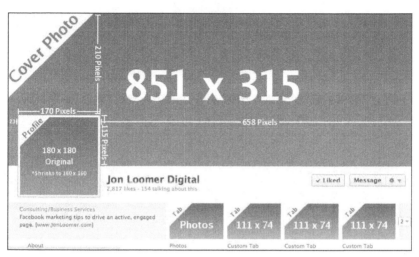

(SkandNet)

Profile Picture

The Profile Picture shows up along with the Cover Image on your Timeline and as the thumbnail next to your posts in user's News Feeds. As mentioned earlier, Profile Pictures should be 180x180. These will shrink to 160x160 on the Timeline and will shrink to about 50x50 as the thumbnail next to your posts in fan's News Feeds. To upload a new Profile Picture hover over the Profile Picture and click on "Edit Profile Picture."

Organizations most often use a logo here, but you can select any image that represents your organization, or change your image based on campaigns or seasonality. Since the image becomes very small in the News Feed, less is often better. For example, too much text will be hard to read. Choose an image that stands out and is recognizable.

Here is an example of a Profile Picture using a logo.

In this example, Ben and Jerry's has updated their Profile Picture to coordinate with a new product launch.

The following Disney example uses a cute iconic image.

Here are all three Pictures as they show up in a user's News Feed.

Macy's

Winter take a toll on your skin? Recover with new skin care arrivals + free online exclusive 10-pc. sampler! http://bit.ly/XUbrD

Ben & Jerry's
We're amped up to re-introduce pints of Coffee, Coffee BuzzBuzzBuzz!
Fairtrade coffee ice cream with espresso bean fudge chunks.

Disney
10 Paperman GIFs to Make You Believe in Destiny: http://di.sn/b9B
Like · Comment · Share · 👍 8,168 💬 96 📋 322 · 11 hours ago · 🌐

Cover Image

The Cover Image is probably the most important element of Timeline. It allows organizations to easily brand the Facebook Page with a large image positioned at the top and center. Here you can get creative. You can use a photo or an original image. The dimensions are 851x315.

NOTE. Here is the link to Facebook cover image restrictions. https://facebook.com/help/search/?q=cover+photo+restrictions

Cover Photos may not contain:

1. Price or purchase information, such as "40% off," or "Download it at our website."
2. Contact information such as web address, email, mailing address or other information intended for your Page's About section.
3. References to user interface elements, such as Like or Share, or other Facebook site features.
4. Calls to action, such as "Get it now," or "Tell your friends."

To get your creative juices flowing, here are a few examples of Cover Images.

BabyCenter uses a simple photo that resonates with the target.

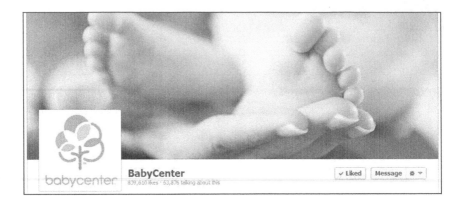

Feiss—Monte Carlo, a lighting company, showcases their light fixtures.

Gap updates their Cover Image regularly based on their current campaign. Note that they have also updated their Profile Photo to coordinate with the campaign.

Starbucks also regularly updates their Cover Image.

Mari Smith, Facebook guru, used the space to recognize reaching 90,000 fans.

TIP: Consider updating your Cover Image periodically. It's a fun way to keep your Timeline fresh and users see the updates in their News Feeds.

Application Tabs/Images

When you create your new Page, you will have two or three tabs. Most organizations will have Photos and Likes, and local organizations will also have a Map. If you have moved an existing Facebook Page to Timeline, you may have other tabs (the way to access applications). Facebook lets you add applications and customize the look and feel of the Tabs.

Adding Tabs

To add tabs (or applications), first click on the down arrow to the right of your existing tabs. Then you will see several blank tab thumbnails. Click on the "+" sign on one of those tabs and you will see a few options. If you plan to have Events, you can click to add that application. To add Videos, choose the Video application.

There are also many non-Facebook applications you can add. We will go into detail about the many applications available and how to add them to your Page in the Facebook Applications chapter.

Re-Arranging Tabs

The Photos tab always stays in the first position, but beyond that you can order the tabs however you like.

To change the order of the tabs, click on the down arrow to the right of your tabs, then click on the pencil, and finally hover down to "Swap position with:" and choose the appropriate tab.

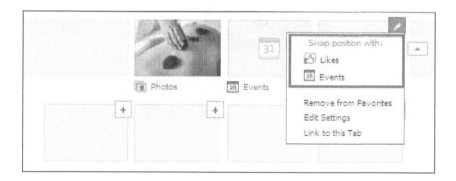

You can customize the name and image for any tabs/applications that you have added. To do this, click on the pencil icon and click on "Edit Settings." There you will see the option to Change the Tab Image and use a Custom Tab Name. The dimensions for tab images are 111x74.

Here are some examples of custom tab names and images.

Likeable Media created About Likeable and Likeable Jobs tabs and customized with images that match the brands look and feel.

BabyCenter added a video tab and a Pinterest tab that includes a co-ordinated image.

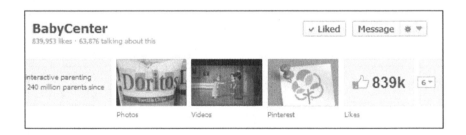

Sephora added Friday specials, Events, Instant Makeover, and created images with Sephora's look and feel.

TIP: Put your most important tabs in the first three positions (after Photos). Some tabs that might deserve priority are a current sweepstakes/promotion, possibly your email opt-in tab, etc. Tabs after the first four are only visible if a person clicks on the down arrow.

Milestones

The last way to customize your Timeline is by adding Milestones. Milestones are important dates for your business, like the date your business was launched, a product was launched, when you moved to a new location or won an award, etc. Here is the handy image we shared earlier, this time with Milestone placement and dimensions.

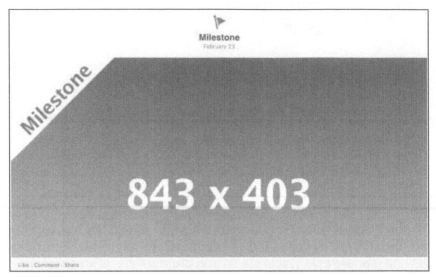

(SkandNet)

Milestones are not seen unless a person scrolls down your Timeline, so they are less important than the other images, but some organizations still like to add these. To add a Milestone, click on "Offer, Event +" and then "Milestone." Then enter the details Facebook requests and upload an image. Note that Milestones can be hidden from your News Feed, if you wish.

Here is an example of a Milestone from Disney's Page.

Launch of Disney Junior, the channel
March 23, 2012

https://facebook.com/DisneyJunior

Like · Comment   4,657 173

Now that your Timeline is ready let's go over posting and then tips for how to launch your Facebook Page.

Posting

It is easy to post on Facebook. First, move your curser to "Write Something" within the status box.

Status Update

To simply post a Status update, enter your copy and click "Post." As we'll talk about later, it's better to post images rather than posting copy alone, whenever possible. To post a photo, image, or video, click on "Photo/Video."

Photo/Video

To post one photo or image click on "Upload Photo/Video," upload it, then write your post. We will talk about tips for writing your posts later. You can also create a Photo Album or use Webcam to create a video to share.

Facebook allows you to post Offers, Events, Milestones, and Questions. To post one of these, click on "Offer, Event +" and then the appropriate type of post.

Offer

Offers used to be available only to local organizations, for in-store redemption, but now they are available to most Facebook Pages. They are not currently available on some smaller Facebook Pages, so it appears there is a minimum number of Likes in order to post Offers. You can create offers that are "In Store Only," "In Store & Online," and "Online Only." We will talk more about Offers and walk you through creating these in the Facebook Advertising chapter.

TIP: Offers are currently free (may change at any time) and good deals are going viral. Make use of Offers now!

Event

If you are hosting an event, click on "Event" and fill in the requested information. After you have created the event, you can add an image by hovering over the calendar icon and clicking on "Add Event Photo."

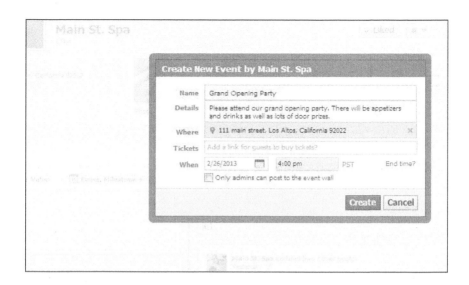

TIP: Consider adding an event as a Facebook Event and also as a link to an information/sign-up page. Seeing the information two ways might be more impactful for your audience.

Milestone

To add a Milestone, first click on "Milestone," then Facebook will ask you to enter the date your business was started. Click on "Milestone" again to add any other Milestones you wish to add. As noted before, you can add images, which we recommend, and hide from the News Feed, if you wish.

Question

You can also create a Question, otherwise known as a Poll. To do this, click on "Question," and then click on "Add Poll Options." Write your question and click "Add an option" to enter an answer. Questions are a fun way to get your audience engaged and can potentially go viral.

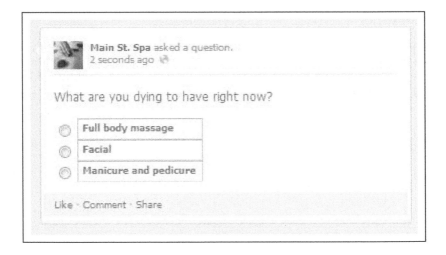

Page Post Targeting

Facebook has recently begun offering the ability to target posts to specific fans. This is only available to Pages with over 5,000 fans at this time. Organizations can target based on personal information including gender, education, age, etc. For larger Pages, this may be a good strategy to increase engagement, since getting your post in front of your ideal audience may increase activity.

The last step in launching a new Facebook Page is to get the word out. It is best to have great posts on the Page so that when people take a look they will like what they see and click "Like." We will go over how to create engaging content in the next chapter, but for now, here are some tips you can keep in mind for how to let your current customers and potential fans know about your Page.

Getting The Word Out

As you probably noticed, Facebook gives you the option to Invite Your Friends. You can do this, and it won't hurt, but many people don't see or ignore these alerts, so this tactic is not particularly effective.

Email

The most basic and very effective tactic for getting the word out about your Facebook Page among your current audience is to send an email. Let them know about your new Facebook Page including the valuable content they will find there.

Even more effective is a contest or sweepstakes enticing your audience to Like the Page. We will talk about the intricacies of running a contest or sweepstakes later.

TIP: Don't underestimate the need to promote your Facebook Page to your current audience. They are more likely to want to "Like" than those with no relationship with your organization. They will also likely be the more active fans on the Page. Others will want to also "Like" the Page if there is a good base of active followers. Send multiple emails to convert them to fans.

Other Promotion

Beyond that, add the Facebook URL or icon everywhere—in a prominent position on your website and blog, to employees email signatures, email/newsletter templates, social media properties, in-store signage, collateral, presentations, business cards, any paid advertising, etc. Also cross-promote your new Facebook Page on any social media properties like a blog, Twitter, LinkedIn Groups, etc.

These tactics should give you an initial bump of Page Likes and ongoing new Likes. More well-known organizations and brands will also see organic growth as people search for the Facebook Pages of their favorite organizations and brands.

Facebook Ad Buys and Sweepstakes/Contests

To increase "Likes" more aggressively, many organizations run Facebook ads or promotions. We will go over options for Facebook ad buys and promotions as well as how to do these in the Advertising on Facebook chapter.

Now that you have created your Facebook Page, customized your Timeline, and know how to post, let's move on to developing the highly valuable content that will make people want to Like and interact with your Page, as well achieve your business objectives.

ACTION ITEMS

- Set up your Facebook Page, if you haven't done so already.

- Customize your Timeline with a Cover Image, Profile Photo, and customized application tab images with your organization's personality and look and feel.

- Promote your Facebook Page to your current audience via email, on your website, on your social media properties, and everywhere else you can—in-store signage, presentations, business cards, etc.

---

3 Creating Great Content

Creating valuable content has always been important on Facebook. Facebook has had an algorithm for deciding who sees which posts, and as more and more people and organizations join Facebook and post, it has become harder to get posts seen by the majority.

Faccbook rcvcalcd in early 2012 that the average post from a brand Page reached only 16% of fans. This percent varies with posts from highly engaging Pagcs reaching a higher percentage of fans, and posts from less engaging Pages reaching fewer fans. Facebook bases delivery of each post on a Page's EdgeRank score, which is influenced by the content, so great content is more important than ever.

EdgeRank

EdgeRank is Facebook's algorithm for determining which posts get delivered to which fans. It is made up of affinity as its most important factor (fan's affinity with the Facebook Page—for example whether they Like or Comment on the posts or visit the Facebook Page), weight (type of content), and time decay (how recently a post was shared). So, it's very important to create great content in order to get the highest EdgeRank possible, and therefore show up in more fan's News Feeds.

Developing Engaging Content

Developing engaging content can take some effort, but it is necessary to build an active community of fans and meet your business objectives. Using common sense and keeping in mind a few tips, you can create great content. We'll provide tips for how to create engaging posts as well as share some examples now, then go over making sure your posts achieve business objectives next.

Highly Valuable

Content must be highly valuable to your audience. Think hard about who the audience is and what type of content would be interesting to them. If you are a larger organization that has personas or has done research on your customers, keep that in mind as you brainstorm what content might be interesting, helpful, and fun to the audience. Smaller companies may interact with customers daily, so keep the customer's needs and wants in mind when thinking about what type of content they would like to get from you.

Facebook Insights, Facebook's analytics tool, is a great place to learn more about your audience and what they like and don't like. We will dive into Insights in Chapter 8, Measuring Success. Posting content that people don't want is the surest way to get people to hide your posts or unlike your Page, so don't make this mistake.

What do fans want to get from you? Fans of a travel site probably want to see pictures of exotic places, fans of a clothing company likely want to see new fashions, fans of a news site want the latest news, and fans of a fitness business might want to see fitness tips. These are simple examples to get the point across to stick to delivering content that is relevant and interesting to your Page audience.

Make sure the content is mostly about the audience and less about you. Some use the 80/20 rule. 80% of posts should be about the audience—content that is really interesting to them and not about you, and 20% of posts should be about you—driving traffic to your site, selling product, etc. We think this is a good rule of thumb, although this may vary significantly based on the type of business, audience, etc.

Image Rich

Create image rich posts. With the new Timeline format, and changes to the EdgeRank algorithm, images are very important. Many believe posts with images are weighted more heavily than those without, and fans are more likely to engage with posts with images, affecting your overall EdgeRank, so include images as much as possible. Along with single images, consider Photo Albums, which also generally do great in terms of engagement. Videos are also good to do sometimes, but harder to create than images, and often not as engaging.

You may be wondering how to find images for your posts. Here are some ideas.

- Take photos yourself. In some cases, these may look great as is. Make them more interesting using a tool like Instagram.

- If your company has a creative department or works with a creative agency, have them create original images or tweak stock images.

- If the posts are blog articles, make sure to include an image on the blog post and share this as an image (vs. a thumbnail with a link) when you post.

- Buy stock photos from sites like iStockPhoto or Shutterstock, or find images with Creative Commons rights from Google or Flickr. If you are securing images for other efforts, re-purpose these.

- There are some great do-it-yourself image creation sites at your disposal like PicMonkey, ShareAsImage, and Someecards.

- Use PowerPoint or PhotoShop to create interesting images.

Short and Clever Copy

The last piece in developing engaging content is to create great copy. In general, copy should be short. A February 2012 study by BlitzLocal found that the posts with 100–119 characters got the most interaction.

Beyond being brief, great copy is also clever to catch a person's attention. And, copy should often include a call to action. Call to actions can be a direct ask for a Like, Comment, or Share, a yes/no question, open-ended question, etc.

Think of each post as a conversation you start with your audience. You can do this by posting highly relevant content, including an image and copy that catch their attention, and asking for a response.

Examples of Engaging Posts

Here are some examples of posts that are valuable to an audience, have great images, and make good use of copy.

Coffee lovers connect with this nice seasonal inspired image. The short copy is a perfect accompaniment to the image. Note the 6,900 Shares on this post. That means that friends of 6,900 fans saw this post. With an average of 229 friends each (Pew Research 5/12), that could mean an additional 1,580,100 people saw this post..impressive!

Jamba Juice is an example of a big company that creates images using an Instagram type tool. The image and copy are timely which resonates with fans and may increase EdgeRank.

Jamba Juice
September 29, 2012

It's turning out to be an endless summer! Let's hang by the beach! #SoCalProblems

Like · Comment · Share   2,904   50   51

Zest Bakery is a small bakery that shares simple photos regularly of their delicious looking bakery items.

Zest Bakery
February 16

I spy glutenfree red velvet cupcakes with cream cheese frosting!

Like · Comment · Share

19 people like this.

Human Erez You had me at red, then there was cream cheese

Jetsetter posts a regular "Daily Moment of Zen" showcasing one of their exotic travel destinations. They keep the copy short and include a link.

The Sephora audience enjoys makeup tips from the pros.

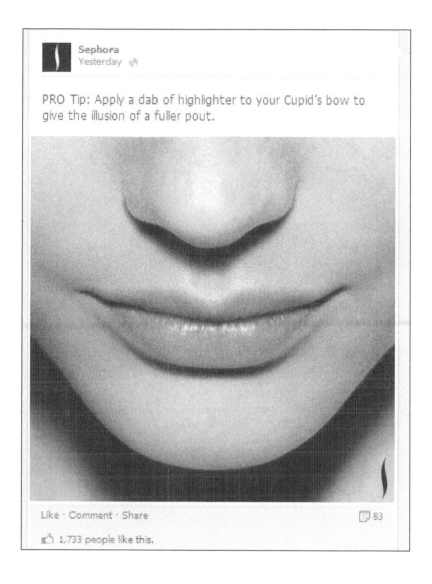

Mint.com regularly shares links to their blog posts on the Facebook Page. Note that they posted the image as a Picture (so it shows up large) versus posting a link (the image would show up as a small thumbnail), and, they include a call to action to respond.

Advance Auto Parts has a Caption This Photo series. They share a fun photo and ask for a caption.

Social Media Examiner shares a screen shot of their blog post if there is no image as part of the post. They also include a question and the name of the person that shared the post to try and start a conversation.

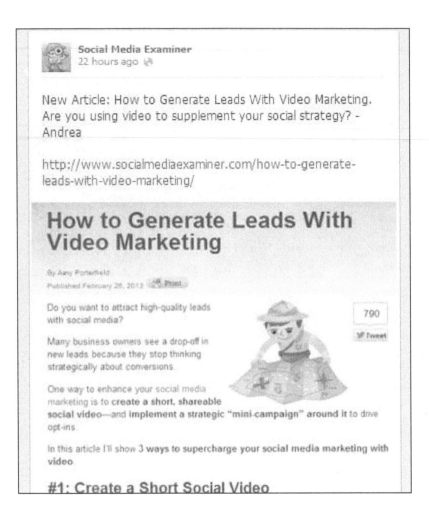

Map Back To Business Objectives

Beyond being valuable and engaging, Facebook posts should map back to your business objectives. Organizations can achieve a variety of objectives on Facebook.

Here are some common objectives that can be achieved on Facebook:

- Staying top of mind

- Increasing awareness

- Increasing brand affinity

- Increasing support for a cause or initiative

- Driving traffic to a website or blog or visits to a physical place of business

- Increasing email list or leads

- Increasing sales (online or physical place of business)

- Decreasing customer support costs

TIP: Choose one or more objectives that are achievable on Facebook and that map back to your business objectives.

Now let's talk about how to utilize content to achieve these objectives.

- Staying top of mind—Frequent relevant posts

- Increasing awareness—Engaging content that gets Liked/Commented on/Shared by fans

- Increasing brand affinity—Visual images that show off your product, helpful posts, or blog articles

- Increasing support for cause or initiative—Compelling images and other content

- Driving traffic to a website/blog or visits to a physical location—Links to content on website or blog articles, sharing reasons to visit a physical store

- Increasing email list or leads—Links to blog articles or special content with a sign up or registration form, sweepstakes or contests

- Increasing sales—Special offers

- Decreasing customer support costs—Answering questions and posting Q&As on your Facebook Page

When To Post

The next important thing to keep in mind for your posting strategy is recency. You want to post when your audience is most likely to be online and engage. There have been many studies done on the best time to post.

Buddy Media shared data on nearly 100 of the company's clients in September 2011. While the information is a bit old, it is well regarded and still used as a benchmark. This research on the company's retail clients found that engagement spikes on Wednesday, with Sunday next in terms of engagement.

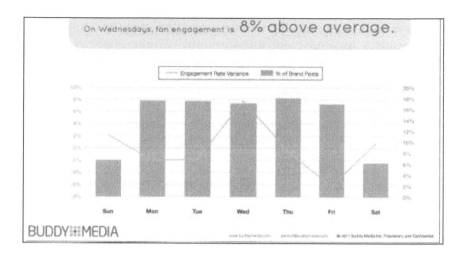

On Wednesdays, fan engagement is 8% above average.

Engagement Rate Variance   % of Brand Posts

Sun   Mon   Tue   Wed   Thu   Fri   Sat

BUDDY⠿MEDIA

This study also found that while the majority of brand posts (89%) are published between 8 a.m. and 7 p.m., posts that are published during less busy times often do well in terms of engagement. According to this data, posts that were published from 8 p.m. to 7 a.m. got 20% higher engagement.

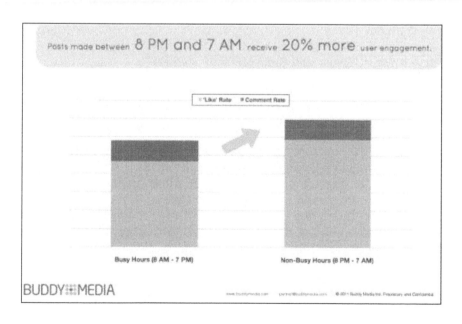

Posts made between 8 PM and 7 AM receive 20% more user engagement.

'Like' Rate   Comment Rate

Busy Hours (8 AM - 7 PM)   Non-Busy Hours (8 PM - 7 AM)

BUDDY⠿MEDIA

An April 2011 study by Buddy Media looked at data from 200 of the company's clients. This data revealed that Thursday and Friday posts got the most engagement. Engagement rates fell about 3.5% below average on Monday through Wednesday, and engagement is lowest on Saturday, at 18% below average. The study dove into engagement by industry. Some notable findings:

- Retail—User engagement spikes on Wednesday and Sunday with Friday being the worst day. Posts made between 8 p.m. and 7 a.m. receive 20% more engagement

- Entertainment—People are most engaged Friday through Sunday

- Automotive—Engagement rates are highest on Sunday

- Business and Finance—Engagement rates spike Wednesday and Thursday and drop sharply on Tuesday and Friday

- Fashion—Engagement peaks on Thursday

- Food and Beverage—Engagement rates are highest on Tuesday and Wednesday with Saturday next in terms of engagement

- Healthcare and Beauty—Engagement rates are highest on Thursday

- Sports—Engagement rates spike on Sunday

- Travel and Hospitality—Highest engagement rates are Thursday and Friday and the lowest engagement rates are Wednesdays and weekends

According to a newer report released in May 2012 by bit.ly, which looked at link click-throughs, links posted from 1–4 p.m. EST get the most click-throughs, with the peak time of the week being Wednesday at 3 p.m. According to this research, Facebook traffic starts to increase at 9 a.m. and fades after 4 p.m. Weekend traffic is lower than weekday. Of course, click-throughs are not always the objective, but this research gives an indication of when people, especially those reading articles and blog posts, are most likely to engage.

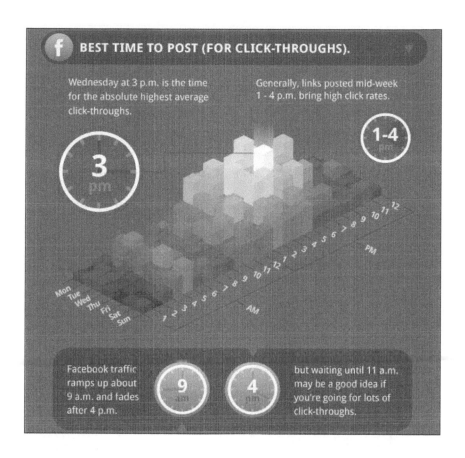

BEST TIME TO POST (FOR CLICK-THROUGHS).

Wednesday at 3 p.m. is the time for the absolute highest average click-throughs.

Generally, links posted mid-week 1 - 4 p.m. bring high click rates.

Facebook traffic ramps up about 9 a.m. and fades after 4 p.m.

but waiting until 11 a.m. may be a good idea if you're going for lots of click-throughs.

In one of the most data intensive research undertakings, Dan Zarella of Hubspot analyzed data from more than 1.3 million posts published on the top 10,000 Facebook Pages. This research was shared in June 2012. He found that posts published on Saturdays and Sundays receive a higher Like percentage than those published during the business week. In addition, content published later in the day gets more Likes and Shares. Shares peak around 6 p.m. EST and Likes peak around 8 p.m.

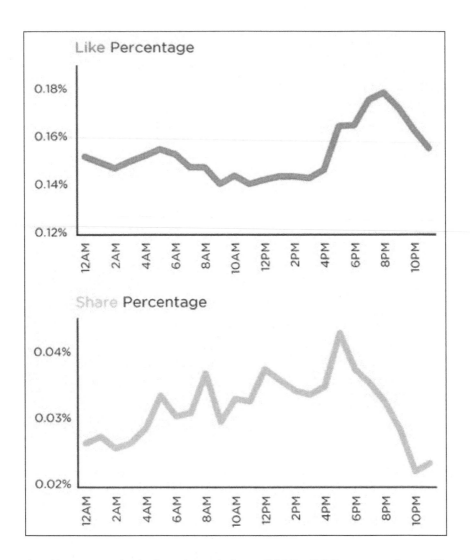

Another recent study, shared June 2012 of 20 companies with college audiences by YesMail, found that Tuesday got the most engagement and 10 p.m. to midnight was an "engagement gold-mine."

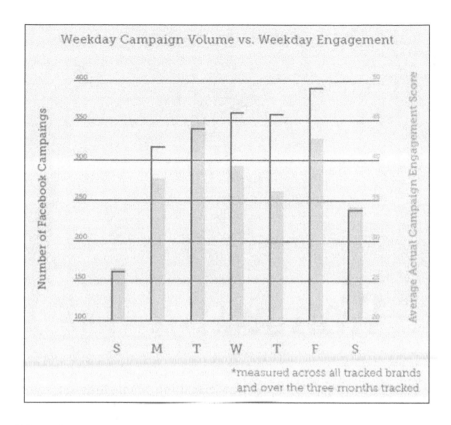

Weekday Campaign Volume vs. Weekday Engagement

Number of Facebook Campaings

Average Actual Campaign Engagement Score

S   M   T   W   T   F   S

*measured across all tracked brands
and over the three months tracked

What these studies all have in common is that their findings all differ! So what should you take away? The bit.ly study looked at click-through rates. Click-throughs are from articles so the content may be more business focused. It might be fair to take away that business audiences might be best reached during normal business hours, especially earlier in the day. The other studies looked more at larger consumer brands. These types of companies might do better posting a little later in the day. And the best day of the week varies by type of company/product. To reach a younger crowd, late at night might be a good time to post. One last piece of data to consider is where your audience is located. If your audience is local, then think about when they will be online. If the audience is across the U.S., then it might be best to focus more on Eastern and Central time zones since the majority of the U.S. population live in those time zones.

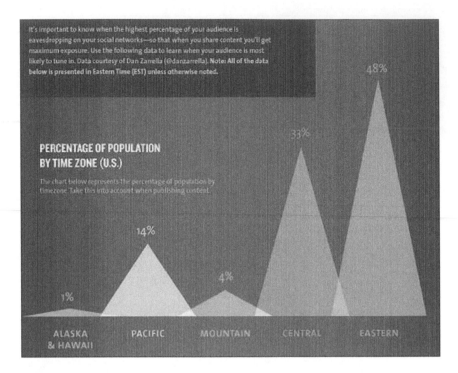

It's important to know when the highest percentage of your audience is eavesdropping on your social networks—so that when you share content you'll get maximum exposure. Use the following data to learn when your audience is most likely to tune in. Data courtesy of Dan Zarrella (@danzarrella). Note: All of the data below is presented in Eastern Time (EST) unless otherwise noted.

PERCENTAGE OF POPULATION BY TIME ZONE (U.S.)

The chart below represents the percentage of population by timezone. Take this into account when publishing content.

48%

33%

14%

4%

1%

ALASKA & HAWAII   PACIFIC   MOUNTAIN   CENTRAL   EASTERN

Use these examples and data as a starting point, then do some testing of different types of content on various days and times and see what does well in terms of reach and engagement.

How Often To Post

It used to be that the rule of thumb was to post at least one time a day. With the announcement that only about 16% of a Page's fans see each post, and increasing News Feed clutter leading to a decreased shelf life, many people advocate posting more frequently. Two to three posts per day seems to be the rule of thumb now. Since the average shelf life of a post is about 4–5 hours, it makes sense to post this often. Organizations that have fans in various time zones should consider that, and schedule posts that will reach all fans. For example, you may need to post throughout the night to reach fans in various areas of the world.

You should still keep engagement and EdgeRank in mind. Only post content that is valuable. If fans don't like your content, it will receive low engagement leading to a lower overall EdgeRank score, decreasing your chances of future posts being shown. So, keep your organizations content creation ability in mind. If it is hard for you to create great content, then post less often with better content.

Creating A Content Calendar

It is helpful to create a content calendar to plan ahead what you will post and when. This is often more efficient and strategic than figuring out what to post day-to-day.

Many organizations do a one-month calendar. Plan posts that engage your audience and map back to your business objectives. Take into account holidays, seasonality, special events, and offers. You don't have to rigidly stick to your calendar. If you come across other content that is great to post, by all means post it. The calendar should be a starting point.

Creating a content calendar is also a helpful way to share your plans with others in your company. To that end, you may also want to color code the objectives each post is meant to achieve.

To increase efficiency, many organizations develop their monthly content, including securing photos and creating images based on the Content Calendar upfront. In cases where a creative department or agency is developing content, this probably makes a lot of sense. This may or may not make sense for smaller organizations that might create content more easily in real-time. Again, in most cases, the Calendar does not need to be rigid. Feel free to make content changes as appropriate.

TIP: Decide how much of your content it makes sense to do upfront. Some organizations create all content upfront. Others have an idea of what they will post, but develop the content day-to-day.

Here is an example of a basic content calendar. This is for Facebook only, but you may want to include your other social media properties so there is a master content plan. While Excel does the trick, you can use other tools like Google Calendar, etc.

Month: February	Monday	Tuesday	Wednesday	Thursday	Friday	Saturday
					1st Health Fun - Exercise All Year Round Senior Flu Article	2nd - Groundhog Day
3rd - Super Bowl	4th Giveaway Ending Soon	5th Giveaway Last Day	6th Weekly Winners Grand Prize winner	7th Health Resolution #6 Buckle Up Did You Know? TBD	8th Health Fun - Exercise Indoors	9th
10th	11th Pre-Teen Vaccination Week	12th Give Kids A Smile Album Health Tip Tuesday - Wash Hands	13th CHI Health Heroes	14th - Valentine's Day Happy Valentine's Day Did You Know? Breastfeeding	15th Health Fun - Red Fruit Park Schedule	16th Flu Article
17th	18th - President's Day Did You Know? Environmental health	19th Health Tip Tuesday - Sugary Beverages CHI Photo Album	20th Health Heroes Solicitation Heart Health Month	21st Did You Know? Aging & Adult Services GH Cross Promotion	22nd Health Fun - Crystal Springs Trail	23rd
24th	25th Reusable Bag Tip 1 - Buy Enough	26th Health Tip Tuesday - Cold & Flu Prevention Reusable Bag Tip 2 - Don't Forget	27th Reusable Bag Tip 3 - Clean Regularly 500 Fans	28th Did You Know? Youth Exercise		

Now that you are creating great content, let's talk about how to manage Facebook and other social media, day-to-day.

ACTION ITEMS

- Create engaging content—Make it valuable to your audience, image rich, and include a call-to-action to engage.

- Determine business objectives you can achieve using Facebook and create a content strategy to meet these objectives.

- Post during time periods you are most likely to reach your audience and they are most likely to engage.

- Create a content calendar to plan your posts.

4 Social Media Management Tools

Many organizations start out posting real-time to Facebook, but that may not be ideal if you want to post at certain times and are not available, or want to be more efficient. If you are using multiple social media properties, you may want one dashboard to simplify efforts. As you get more sophisticated with your social media efforts, you will want to consider more comprehensive tools.

There are many Facebook management and social media management options.

Facebook Scheduled Posts

Facebook recently released the capability to schedule posts. This functionality is available within the sharing tool on a Page. To do this, choose the type of post, click on the clock icon, choose the date and time that you want the post to appear, and click "Schedule." Posts can be scheduled up to six months in advance. You can also add posts for dates in the past using this method. The benefit of scheduling using Facebook's tool is that many believe Facebook gives a lower EdgeRank to posts scheduled via third party tools.

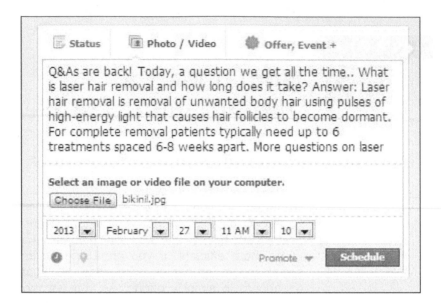

To see your scheduled posts, click on "Edit Page" and "Use Activity Log." Click on the down arrow to change the time, publish immediately, or cancel the post.

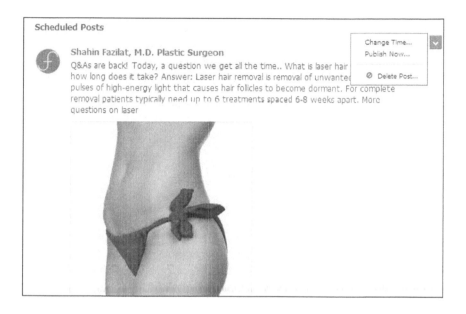

Facebook's scheduler is a great option for posting to Facebook. It makes it easy to schedule your posts in advance at the exact times you want them to show. Since this is a Facebook tool, there is no penalty.

Facebook Pages Manager iPhone Application

To post and manage a Facebook Page on the go, Admins can use the Facebook Pages Manager iPhone application. This application was released in May 2012 and greatly improves the functionality from the previous application. Using this tool, you can do most of what you can do from the desktop Facebook Page. You can create status updates and posts that include photos, schedule posts, respond to Comments or Page Posts, create Promoted Posts, create Offers, and also view Insights, Admins, and Page Settings. It is easy to toggle between Facebook Pages. It remains hard to post links or images that are not on your phone.

TIP: As this book goes to print Facebook has just launched an application for Android users.

Third Party Social Media Management Tools

If you are posting to multiple social networks and want to consolidate efforts, or want to integrate more capabilities like listening to conversations about your business on Facebook or other social media properties, responding, and analytics, then consider third party tools.

Here is a list of several popular third party social media management tools with prices and capabilities.

HootSuite
http://hootsuite.com/

Free to $9.99/month (or more for enterprise solutions). The free version allows you to manage up to five social profiles (Facebook, Twitter, etc.), schedule posts, and run basic reports. From one dashboard, you can monitor and respond to activity as well as post on Facebook and other properties including Twitter, LinkedIn, FourSquare, Google+, and WordPress. The Pro version, at $9.99/month allows the basic capabilities as well as unlimited profiles, two users, organization management (assigning messages, etc.), and Facebook Insights and Google Analytics integration. HootSuite is a very popular basic social media management tool, and its integration with Google Analytics makes it possible to track traffic and performance by campaigns. HootSuite is a very popular and inexpensive option.

Sprout Social
https://sproutsocial.com/

$9 to $99/month. Sprout Social has a very nice user interface that allows you to manage multiple divisions or organizations and social media properties easily. From the dashboard, you can monitor and respond to messages, view Twitter feeds, schedule posts, listen and find people to follow (for Twitter), assign tasks to team members, and run reports. The Facebook report is made up of data from Facebook Insights and includes relevant information (some that is not easily found in Facebook Insights) in a nice visual format that is easily downloaded to a PDF. The $59/month version includes Google Analytics integration. The $99/month version includes management of up to 100 profiles. Drawbacks of Sprout Social are that the reports are not customizable and Sprout Social only supports Facebook, Twitter, and LinkedIn currently. Sprout Social has a nice interface, is easy to use, and relatively inexpensive.

Postling
https://www.postling.com/

$1/month trial. $5/month for up to 5 accounts. $3/month for each additional account. Postling is a dashboard for social media management across multiple platforms. It supports Facebook, Twitter, LinkedIn, blogs, Flickr, YouTube, and review sites like Yelp and TripAdvisor, making it a good choice for local or service organizations. Postling makes it easy to monitor social media with a daily email, and inbox with all activity. It also allows posting and scheduling to all properties. Some drawbacks are that Postling does not have a workflow management system and Analytics are limited.

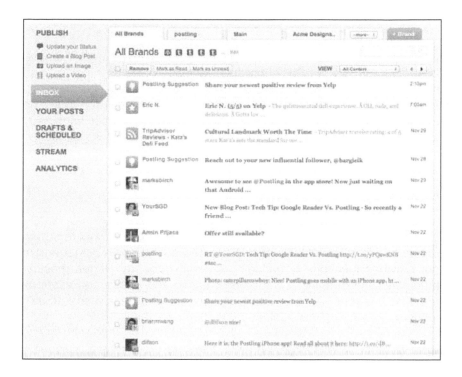

There are other interesting tools to consider.

Buffer
http://bufferapp.com/

Buffer is a tool to easily share articles as well as post to your social media accounts. You can add a number of posts for a timeframe and set times to post, or Buffer will spread out the posts and share at appropriate times. This tool is very useful for scheduling to Twitter and also appropriate for some organizations on Facebook.

Businesses with related products are also coming out with broader social media management tools. Two of these include Vertical Response and Wildfire.

Vertical Response Social
http://verticalresponse.com/social-media-marketing

$9/month when paired with any other Vertical Response product. $18/month for only the Social product. Includes up to 6 properties and 300 posts/month. This can be a handy tool for companies that use Vertical Response for email and want to consolidate dashboards. The product allows you to schedule, respond, and easily post third party content on Facebook, Twitter, and LinkedIn. The tool includes limited analytics.

Wildfire
http://www.wildfireapp.com/

Contact Wildfire for Pro and Enterprise plans. Wildfire is a well regarded Facebook promotions application. Their new social media management tool provides functionality including creating property Pages, posting and scheduling, running promotions, creating and analyzing Facebook ads, and analytics. An interesting component of its analytics is that it benchmarks your results against the industry average.

For organizations with larger budgets, there are more robust tools.

Raven Tools
http://raventools.com/social-media-tools/

$99/month for Pro and $249/month for Agency. Includes standard social media management functionality like scheduling and workflow management, as well as customized reporting, seo tools, Google AdWords integration, and a CRM system.

Argyle Social
http://argylesocial.com/

$300/month for single user, $400/month for social media marketing teams, $1,000/month for larger teams. Argyle Social includes the basics like posting, scheduling, and workflow management for Facebook, Twitter and LinkedIn. It also measures the most important metrics for an organization, including conversions, sales, and social ROI.

For organizations that require more powerful solutions, there are additional options. These tools are more expensive, usually over $1,000 a month, and require negotiating with a sales person. These are robust tools with more capabilities and flexibility. We won't go into detail here, but some tools to consider for organizations looking for a more robust social media management tool are Adobe's Social Publishing tool (formerly Context Optional), Hearsay Social, Buddy Media (owned by SalesForce), and Involver or Vitrue (Owned by Oracle).

Before you choose a tool, think about your objectives, what properties you want to manage, and required functionality. Most are either free or offer a free trial so you can try one or more tools. As always, the space changes constantly so these tools will change and new options will become available. Keep your eyes open to make sure you are using the best tool for your business.

ACTION ITEM

- Choose the social media management tool that is the most appropriate for your business considering capabilities needed and budget.

---

5 Community Management

Now that you have your Facebook Page up, are creating valuable content, and have some management processes in place, it's time to talk about how to manage the activity of the community.

Let's clarify what community management is. We refer to community management as monitoring the Facebook Page and responding to questions or comments, encouraging conversation, handling negative fan comments, and acting in the case of a crisis or major relevant event. The community manager is there to be the Facebook voice for the organization.

Who Should Manage

The person or team responsible for doing the community management on a Facebook Page differs by organization. For a one-person business, it will be the owner that manages the community. For small organizations, there might be one person or a couple of people designated to take on this role. Larger organizations might designate one person or a small team. The Community Managers will likely be in the Marketing department, but may also have other roles in the organization. Some organizations outsource community management (and sometimes all Facebook management) to outside consultants or agencies. Most importantly, designate a person/s for this role that is/are helpful and can speak in the company voice. Designate times that each person is responsible for the Page if there is more than one person, and be clear on responsibilities.

TIP: Choose a person (or more than one person) to manage your Facebook Community that understands the business well, is friendly, likes to engage with the audience, and specify who is responsible for managing the community at all times.

How To Be A Good Community Manager

A good community manager interacts regularly with the Page fans in a helpful manner. They are present and respond to comments, engage the audience, handle unhappy customers, and moderate and delete inappropriate posts.

Respond

An important role of a community manager is to respond to fan questions and comments that require a response. If a person asks a question, respond to them. Think about if you were to go into a store and ask a question. You would expect a response. The same goes on a Facebook Page. People will think you don't care and may get upset if you don't respond. Selfishly, any comments fans make are shared with their friends, so you want to provide a response and encourage further conversation. These responses are often handled by the Community Manager, and sometimes delegated to other teams such as Customer Support, etc. If you delegate, make sure there is a prompt response.

In this example from the Social Media Examiner Facebook Page, Grant's question is answered in under 15 minutes. Social Media Examiner tags the fan so that the person is alerted. And, they end all posts/Comments with the responder's name so fans feel like they are interacting with real people.

In this example from Red Tricycle's Facebook Page, Red Tricycle helps resolve the fan's problem promptly.

In addition to responding to public Comments on the Facebook Page, also respond to Private Comments from fans. While these are not visible to everyone, you want to provide good customer support for happy fans and stronger affinity with your organization.

TIP: Respond to any questions promptly. The person that asked will be grateful and more likely to do business with you or recommend to a friend.

Encourage Conversation

Along the same lines, an important role of the person managing the Facebook community is to encourage conversation. You want to encourage conversation to create a feeling of community among your fans, increase affinity with your brand, and increase virality, since Comments are seen by fan's friends. You can do this by periodically commenting as the Page.

In this case from the ThredUp Facebook Page, ThredUp jumps in and starts a conversation with a fan. Fans like hearing from the Facebook Page and are likely to comment more in the future as well as have stronger affinity with the Page and business.

TIP: Jump in regularly to encourage conversation. You are building affinity with the other person and your organization, encouraging others to converse, and increasing your reach virally as more and more people get involved in the conversation.

Handle Negative Comments

All organizations get negative comments once in a while. It is a natural tendency to want to delete these, but that is often not the best way to handle these. If you do that, the fans that post legitimate comments may get upset, and others may notice the lack of any negative comments and not trust the Page as fully. People expect some negative comments.

What is important is how you handle these. For legitimate negative comments, you want to respond quickly with an apology and what you are doing to rectify the situation. If the information might be helpful to others, you can respond with all information in a Comment. If it is better to respond privately, you can respond by letting the person know to Private Message, or provide an email or phone number for the person to contact.

Always make sure to look for and respond to negative Private Comments.

Let Your Fans Do The Work

As your Facebook Page gets larger and fans start to feel a part of the community, they will start to jump in and respond to comments, answer other's questions, and defend negative posts. This is great. This really increases the sense of community, people trust responses from those outside of the organization, any posts from fans get seen by their friends, and this saves you time.

Here is an example of a fan responding to a negative post on Starbuck's Facebook Page.

Syl Via

It's very annoying when you have free rewards and they mysteriously disappear. With all the money spent at your store you guys should be more considerate of the rewards your clients earn.

Like · Comment · 2 hours ago

👍 2 people like this.

 Michelle Walsh Are you sure that they're not so much mysteriously disappearing but rather expiring? I'm just asking because not everyone is aware that they expire.
about an hour ago · Like · 👍 2

 Gina 'Verburg' Hiskes I've never had a problem using a reward in 30 days.
about an hour ago via mobile · Like

TIP: Contrary to what we said earlier about responding promptly, as you get a larger fan base you may want to delay a response sometimes and let others respond for you.

Handle Inappropriate Posts and Spam

We said earlier that it is ok and expected to get some negative posts. But what if a fan posts negative posts over and over, posts inappropriately, or posts spam. You need to take care of these situations so they don't annoy other fans or negatively affect your organization. If a person is posting regular negative comments, and you have not been able to make them stop with your great customer service, you can ban them. Likewise, if a fan posts inappropriate Comments or posts or irrelevant Spam, you can delete this. To delete a Comment, hover over the right side. You will see an X and "Hide as Spam." When you do this you will be given the options to also "report it as abusive" and "ban" the user.

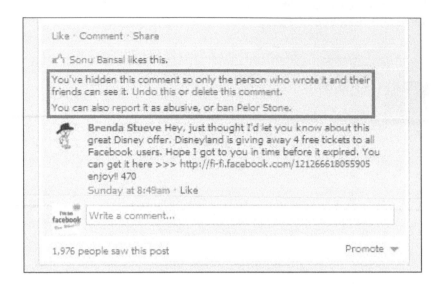

To delete Page Posts, hover over the right side of the post and you will see the option to "Remove." When you click on "Remove," you will be prompted to "Delete." When you do this, you will be given the option to "Delete and Ban User."

Helpful Tools

To help you stay on top of what is happening on the Facebook Page and to respond promptly, there are a couple helpful tools.

Facebook Notifications

Set your Page Notifications to send an email every time a fan posts, Comments, or messages the Page.

To do this, click on "Edit Page" and then "Manage Notifications." Select to send email notifications of Page activity.

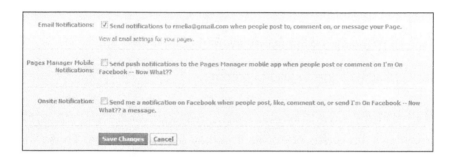

Note that Facebook email notifications are not always reliable, so other activity alert methods are also available.

HyperAlerts

A very handy tool that will alert you to any activity on a Page is HyperAlerts http://www.hyperalerts.no. HyperAlerts will send you close to real-time email alerts for any posts or Comments on your Facebook Page. This makes it easy to make sure you are on top of any activity that might require action.

TIP: HyperAlerts is a great tool to alert you to any activity on your Facebook Page.

Social Media Management Tools

For Pages where there are multiple people involved and you want to delegate tasks and keep track of responses, several of the social media management tools mentioned earlier include community management functionality.

By using popular tools like HootSuite and Spout Social, you can delegate tasks to other team members or send an email of the post that requires a response, and then keep track of actions taken by the team.

Planning For Special Circumstances

You may want to plan for how your organization will handle any special circumstances in advance. These might include a crisis such as a natural disaster, a PR crisis, or major events that could affect your Page like winning a large sports event (sports team), etc.

Here are some steps to take to prepare.

Plan Ahead

Brainstorm any crises or events that may affect your Page. These will vary greatly by Page and some types of organizations may not be affected by crises or events. Some types of crises and events to think about are natural disasters, a PR crisis like bad press or major negative social media attention, and planned events like entertainment events, sporting events, elections, local gatherings, etc.

For each possible special circumstance, develop a handling process. You may want to include:

- Who will be contacted

- Potential posts (consider creating content ahead of time)

- Who has final approval of any posts

- Who will respond and moderate

Update management, marketing teams, or anyone involved with the plans.

Be Timely

Plan to act in a timely manner. The longer you wait in a crisis the more out of control the situation may become. Here is an example from Chick-fil-A's Facebook Page.

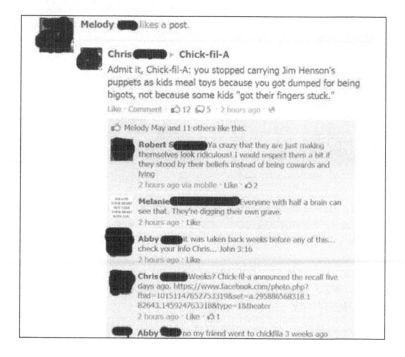

Capitalize on Events

Think beyond managing your organization's crises to how you can support your community or even capitalize on outside events. In the case of a crisis such as a natural disaster, think of how you can support your community. You may be able to provide information, tips, or resources.

In the case of a positive event like a sports team winning a major event, elections, entertainment events, etc. affected Pages should be ready to respond and handle any additional activity.

The San Francisco Giants were prepared and posted this message minutes after winning the game.

In summary, make sure to designate a community manager/s, provide great support, encourage conversation, and be prepared for major negative or positive events.

Have fun and enjoy the community. If you want the best for your community, that sentiment will show through with a more loyal and engaged community.

ACTION ITEMS

- Choose a community manager or team of community managers and specify their roles and times when they are responsible for managing the community.

- Create guidelines for how to respond to questions and comments, how to react to negative posts and spam, and what to do in a crisis or major event (and when others should be involved).

- Choose tools to manage activity on the Facebook Page.

- Work towards building an engaged community!

---

6 Advertising On Facebook

Facebook paid advertising products can be used effectively for various objectives. Facebook ads are a great way to increase Page Likes. They can also be used to increase engagement on a Page or to drive traffic off of Facebook. It used to be very inexpensive to advertise on Facebook. Now that there are many more advertisers, there is more competition and prices have increased, but it often still makes sense to advertise on Facebook.

There are a variety of ad products, and with the increasing pressure to monetize since Facebook went public, expect to see more and more ad products rolled out.

Facebook Ad Products

Facebook ads can be organized by those that appear outside of the News Feed, within the News Feed, as part of search, and on mobile devices. Some ad products appear in more than one of these categories. We will go through the various products.

First, let's go over those that appear outside of the News Feed.

Marketplace Ads

These have been around for a long time and are the most common Facebook ad product. They appear on the right sidebar next to a user's News Feed, on a user's profile Page, or on other pages within Facebook. These do-it-yourself ads can be purchased on a cost-per-click (CPC) or a cost-per-thousand (CPM) basis.

They can be a standard ad that includes copy and an image, or Facebook's social endorsement option, a Sponsored Story. There is no minimum spend.

Marketplace ads can be used to increase Page Likes, increase engagement on a Page, and to drive people off of Facebook. They are easy to create and we will walk you through how to launch a Marketplace ad, as well as give some best practices, later in this chapter.

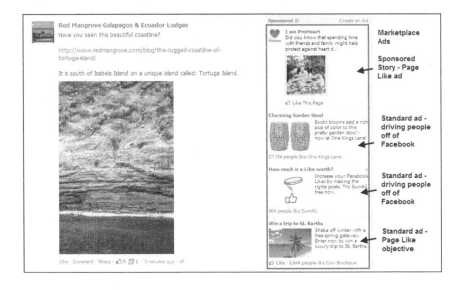

TIP: Standard ads and Sponsored Stories are popular ad types that can be very effective.

Premium Ad

These ads appear exclusively on the right sidebar next to a user's News Feed. The difference between these ads and Marketplace ads is that Premium ads show up alone, whereas Marketplace ads often show up with as many as six other advertisers. Premium ads are sold on a CPM basis, are purchased through an ad sales rep, and require a minimum spend. Premium ads are typically sold to large advertisers with big budgets.

Facebook Exchange

Facebook Exchange (FBX) is cookie based ad retargeting. These are ads that show up in the right sidebar, similar to a Marketplace ad or premium ads. They are targeted to user's who have been exposed to an advertiser's message and often been to the advertiser's site. These ads are being tested as this book is written and will be able to be purchased through ad resellers and on a CPM or CPC basis. There will likely be a minimum spend. These ads will likely be sold primarily to large advertisers with big budgets.

Logout Ad

This is an 850x400 ad currently being tested that is served when a user logs out of Facebook. It is sold on a flat fee basis to large advertisers, and rumored to cost up to $700k/day. These ads tend to have a post that appears as a status update and a video.

Facebook also has several ad options that appear within a user's News Feed.

Promoted Posts

Facebook offers the option of promoting a current Page post. This ad option was introduced soon after the company announced that a typical post only reaches about 16% of the Page's fans. Promoted posts are available to Pages with 400 to 100,000 fans. The Page Admin selects a post that is less than three days old and selects the budget and the corresponding number of people to reach.

Initially, Promoted Posts targeted a Page's fans, and recently Facebook has added the ability to target fan's friends. While some argue posts should be delivered to all of a Page's fans, since they don't, Promoted Posts are an effective way to get important posts into more fan's (and now fan's friends) News Feeds.

HubSpot

Prove the ROI of your Facebook marketing efforts. Start attracting real customers today!

Free ebook: How to Attract Customers with Facebook
offers.hubspot.com

Download free ebook: How to attract customers with facebook

Like · Comment · Share · 👍 8,293 💬 291 📄 261 · ⤴ · Sponsored

TIP: Promoted Posts are an inexpensive way to get important posts in front of all of your fans (and their friends). Post your content without promoting first so fans that see the post organically don't see "Sponsored," then do the Promoted Post for more reach.

Facebook Offers

This is a free Page post that appears as an Offer. Offers were initially available to local organizations only, but are now available to all organizations. Pages can create an offer that includes a thumbnail image, headline, terms, number of redemptions, and expiration date. Once a fan clicks on the Offer, it shows up in their News Feed, giving the Offer the potential to go viral. Offers show up to desktop as well as mobile users, making Offers a great way to reach mobile users.

TIP: To increase reach of an Offer make it a Promoted Post.

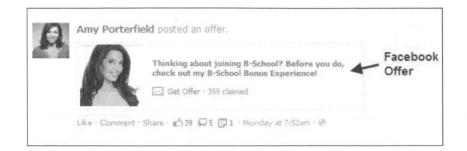

Brand new (and possibly still being tested) are Offers in the right sidebar.

Since Facebook Offers are free and they have the opportunity to go viral, there is no harm in giving them a try.

Facebook has been slow to build out or monetize search, but their first ad product, called Sponsored Results, is currently being tested.

Sponsored Results

Currently being tested by only a few advertisers, an advertiser's Page, app, etc. comes up before organic search results when a person types in selected terms. This ad product is not widely available at this time, but Facebook says this will likely be available on a self-serve basis soon. Mark Zuckerberg recently announced that Facebook has 1 billion search queries a month (compared to Google's 100 billion/month) and also announced the company envisions searches like "What sushi restaurants have my friends gone to in NY in the last six months and Liked?" Expect Facebook to focus on its search options given the vast user data Facebook has available and the need to monetize.

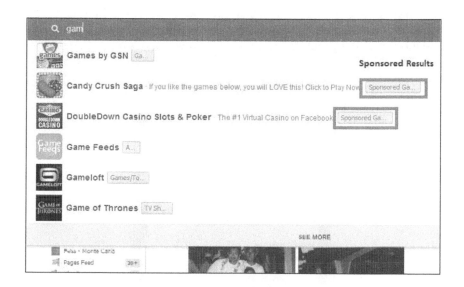

TIP: Keep your eyes open for when Sponsored Results are more widely available. Facebook search is not very good so Sponsored Results might be a great way to help people find your Page.

In May 2012, Facebook announced that time spent on Facebook mobile surpassed time spent on the website. To capitalize on this opportunity, and offset potential revenue declines from less web use, Facebook has announced a couple mobile ad products. Look for more ad products in the future as mobile is a major priority for the company.

The first ad product, announced in June 2012, was Sponsored Stories for mobile. Recently, in August 2012, Facebook announced News Feed Ads for developers.

Sponsored Stories for Mobile

These Sponsored Stories are just like the regular Sponsored Stories except they show up in a mobile user's News Feed. Early data shows that they are doing very well compared to the desktop version. According to AdParlor, click-through-rates are 15x higher on mobile ads than desktop ads and clicks are 30% cheaper. In this study, conversion rates were 16% less, but the higher click-through-rate and cheaper cost more than make up for the lower conversion rate.

(TechCrunch)

TIP: Mobile Page Like Stories are really impactful and generally very effective at increasing Likes inexpensively.

News Feed Ads for Developers

This ad is currently in a small private beta and is available to Android and ioS application developers. When a user clicks, they are taken to purchase pages. It is purchased on a CPC.

As with all things Facebook, the company makes changes to its ad products all the time, so watch for changes to current ad products as well as new ad products.

How To Do An Ad Buy

Several of Facebook's ad options can be created via the self-service platform. Here you can create a Marketplace ad that consists of either a typical ad (copy and image) or Sponsored Story. Sponsored Stories can run solely on mobile devices. Here are step-by-step directions for creating an ad using the self-service platform.

1. Go to https://www.facebook.com/ads and click on "Create an Ad" in the upper right hand corner.
2. You can either advertise a Facebook Page or advertise a website off of Facebook. All Facebook Pages that you are an Admin of will be listed. Select one if you want to advertise a Page or type in the URL of an external website.

Standard Ads

The following instructions will walk you through creating a standard ad that promotes a Facebook Page. Creating a standard ad that drives people off Facebook is almost the same so we will give directions for how to do that next.

3. Facebook will ask "What do you want to promote?" You can select the Facebook Page or a specific post. Assuming you want to promote the Facebook Page, select that.
4. At this point, you can select whether you want to create a new ad or a Sponsored Story.

If you select the new ad option, here is where you provide the details.

5. Enter text (90 character limit) and upload an image (100x72). You cannot enter a title; rather Facebook will use the title of your Facebook Page.

TIP: Generally, clear and concise copy that explains benefits works best. Include a call to action to Like, click, etc.

---

6. Then select "Landing View" (where you want a person to land when they click on your ad). Facebook will list all the tabs on the Page, for example, Timeline, Photos, Events, and any additional tabs like sweepstakes, etc. If the objective is to increase Likes, Timeline is probably the best choice. If the objective is to increase Event registrations, choose that tab, or for a sweepstakes/contest choose that tab.

Next, choose the targeting.

7. For location, leave United States selected if the campaign is targeting the entire U.S. Or you can target another country/ies or by State, City or Zip code. Targeting by geography is great for local organizations, but note making the target too small will sometimes lead to delivery problems and often an increased cost per click.

8. Next, select age and gender.

9. Then select interests. Precise Interests is where you can target based on what a person has listed as an interest on their Timeline. It is pulled from their interests, activities, education, job title, Pages they have Liked, or Groups they belong to. For example, using the spa Facebook Page we created earlier, we can target people who like spas, facials, and massages, as well as people that have Liked similar spa Facebook Pages.

10. Then select who you would like to see the ad. You can select Anyone, Only people connected to the Page, Only people not connected to the Page, Advanced Connection Targeting (People who are or are not connected to an app, event, etc.), or Friends of Connections (friends of people that have Liked a Page).

11. Brand new to the Facebook ads creation process is Objective. The options are to "Show this to people who are most likely to like my Page" or "Show this to people who are most likely to click on my ad or Sponsored Story." Like the Page gets cost per thousand (CPM) pricing and click on the ad or Sponsored Story gets cost per click (CPC) pricing. In the past, advertisers could simply choose CPM or CPC. You will likely need to test and see which buying method is the most efficient. In this example, new Likes is the objective so try buying both ways and see which gets a lower cost per Like.

12. Create a Campaign Name and Campaign Budget. The budget can be per day or per campaign. It is generally fine to select per campaign as Facebook usually delivers pretty evenly over the campaign time period. If you want to increase or decrease the spend on certain days, select the per day option and change as necessary.

13. Finally, click "Place Order." Now you have one ad created. Facebook automatically optimizes within a campaign, so it's usually recommended to create multiple ads that Facebook can choose between. If you want to get sophisticated and test variables, then it is necessary to create multiple campaigns with multiple ads within those campaigns.

TIP: Give your ad a name that makes sense by hovering over the ad and clicking on the pencil. To create additional similar ads, click on an ad and then "Create A Similar Ad." Then click on pencil to change the name.

To drive people off Facebook, follow the exact same directions except enter the website URL instead of choosing a Facebook Page. When you create an ad that drives people to a website or landing page, you can create a headline whereas for a Facebook Page, Facebook enters the Page name as the headline.

Sponsored Stories

Now let's talk about Sponsored Stories, the second self-serve option. There are two types of Sponsored Stories—Page Like Stories and Page Post Stories.

Page Like Story

Page Like Stories are a simple ad that mentions that a person Likes a Page. They are delivered to friends of fans of a Facebook Page. Since they mention a person's friend in the ad, they employ social proof to attempt to persuade a person to Like a Page.

Page Like Stories can be very effective at increasing Likes. To create this type of ad, select "Stories about their friends liking xx" in the "People Will See" section. To do a Page Like Story, the Facebook Page needs to have fans, the more the better.

Page Like Sponsored Stories usually run on a user's desktop computer, but can also run on a mobile device. The mobile ads really stand out and are very effective at increasing Likes. To target Facebook's mobile users go to Interests, and within the "Broad Categories" section, select "Mobile Users (All)."

(AllFacebook)

Page Post Story

The second Sponsored Story option is the Page Post Story. This ad displays a current Page post. It is great for increasing engagement on a Facebook Page. Some advertisers use this post as a way to share video in an ad, something that is not otherwise possible.

To set up a Page Post Story just select "A specific post on xx" in the "What do you want to promote?" section. Then select the post to promote. You can select to include just the post or also include a person's friends that Like the post. To include friends, you need a larger fan base.

Since Facebook updates ad products and changes their interface constantly, these instructions will undoubtedly change, but hopefully they will get you started and you will be able to navigate any changes.

Ad Buy Suggestions

Different tactics work well for different advertisers, but here are some standard tips that often work well across various types of organizations and industries.

- Create multiple ads within a Campaign. For test results that are more than directional, create different campaigns for each variable (budget needs to be larger for multiple campaigns).

- Test different images. Close-ups of smiling people often do well. Images should catch a person's attention.

- Simple clear copy often does well.

- Including a Like call to action works well, if that is the goal.

- Page Like Stories are working very well, especially on mobile, and Offers are showing a lot of promise.

- TEST TEST TEST—including testing seasonality and buying on a CPM vs. CPC

Lastly, as a result of Facebook's constant changes as well as variables outside of anyone's control, there are times when campaigns seem to do really well and times when they don't. This may be due to Facebook serving more or less ads, the number of advertisers, or people having more or less time on their hands, among other reasons. The point is, if your campaign does really well, great, advertise more. If not, consider waiting and trying again at a different time.

How To Do A Promoted Post

It is easy to create a Promoted Post. Follow these simple directions.

Promoted Post

1. Select a post on your Page that you want to promote, go to the bottom of the post, and click "Promote."
2. Select whether you want the ad to go to "People who like your Page" or "People who like your Page and their friends."
3. Select the appropriate budget.
4. You can click on the wheel icon to change the payment method.

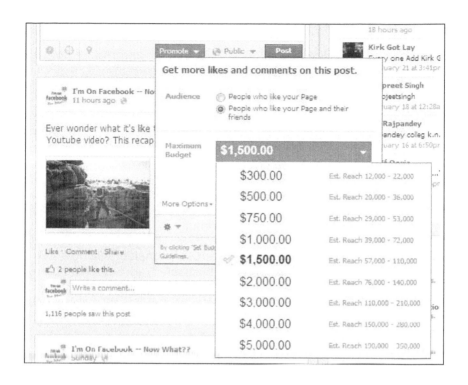

TIP: A Promoted Post will run for three days, so start it based on the three days you want it to run. For example, if Thursday is your best day you may want it to run Wednesday through Friday.

ACTION ITEMS

- Look at your News Feed on your computer and mobile phone and notice the various ad products.

- Go to where you can set up the various self-service ads— **https://www.facebook.com/ads** for standard ads and Sponsored Stories, on the bottom right of a post for Promoted Posts, and within the status update area for Offers—and see how these ads are created.

- If appropriate, set up a Facebook ad buy. You can set up a small test buy for very little money. $50 or so will allow you to test the ad product and get you some learning.

- If you are a current Facebook advertiser, consider testing a new ad product or creating more sophisticated ad buys (standard ads) for better results.

7 Sweepstakes And Contests

Sweeptakes and contests can be used very effectively on Facebook to achieve various business objectives. First, let's go over the difference. In a sweepstakes winners are chosen by chance, and in a contest winners are chosen by judges. Sweepstakes are often a great way to increase Page Likes. They are also great for collecting email addresses. Contests are a great way to get users to engage with a brand. They can also be used effectively to increase Page Likes and gain email addresses, but because of the higher barrier to entry, volume is often lower than for sweepstakes.

It's important to know that Facebook has strict guidelines regarding sweepstakes and contests. Here are the guidelines (which can change at any time so make sure to check Facebook for the most recent guidelines in advance of a promotion) https://facebook.com/page_guidelines.php.

Probably the most important guideline is that sweepstakes and contests must be administered within "Apps on Facebook.com." The easiest way to do this is by using an approved 3rd party provider. It is also possible to develop your own app. Another important guideline is that user's can be made to Like a Page to gain entry, but interacting with a post cannot be a condition of entry. You have probably noticed that there are many Pages running sweepstakes or contests that are not adhering to these rules. They risk the Page being shut down, so it's not worth taking that risk.

TIP: Don't run a sweepstakes or contents on Facebook without using a 3rd party application or you risk Facebook shutting down your Page.

To get your creative juices running, here are a few examples of sweepstakes and contests.

Sweepstakes And Contests Examples

Rubbermaid's Fall Prep Kit Sweepstakes—In this Sweepstakes, Rubbermaid is giving away its own products, which keeps the cost of running this sweepstakes very low as well as attracts people that like Rubbermaid products.

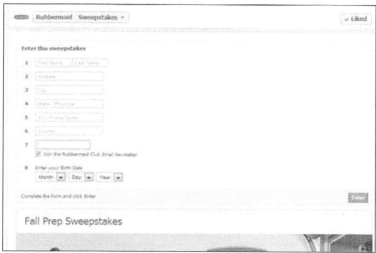

BOB Stroller Giveaway—BOB strollers are expensive so giving one away is a great incentive to get parents to enter. BOB used Wildfire to run this promotion, including social elements that allow people to "Share to my Wall" and invite Facebook friends as part of the entry process.

Benefit's Beauty Best...Or Bust? Contest—Benefit encouraged fans to submit a photo of their best or worst beauty moment in a contest to win a trip to Los Angeles, tickets to a taping of Fashion Police, a meet and greet with the hosts, a Macy's shopping spree, and $500 of Benefit products. Since the judges will select a winner from the photos with the most entries, entrants are given incentive to get their friends to come to the Facebook Page to vote, doing Benefit's marketing for them.

Scholastic Reading Club Sweepstakes—Scholastic ran this fun scratch and win sweepstakes to encourage sign ups and collect email addresses.

Red Tricycle/Old Navy Gift Card Sweepstakes—This sweepstakes encouraged social sharing, increased Likes of Red Tricycle and Old Navy Facebook Pages, and collected email addresses.

Promotion Best Practices

Here are a few promotion suggestions and best practices:

- Select the appropriate promotion type. As a rule of thumb, consider a sweepstakes for gaining Likes, collecting email addresses, and generating excitement. Consider contests for increasing engagement, and to a lesser extent, gaining Likes and collecting email addresses.

- Choose prizes that are appealing to your audience. This could be your product or something that is relevant. iPads and trips are common prizes that appeal to many, but it is best to choose prizes even more relevant to your target to attract the right people.

- Make it the right length. Make your sweepstakes or contest long enough to get enough entrants, but short enough that it still generates enthusiasm. A month is an approximate good length. Contests often have multiple phases so they sometimes require a longer duration.

- Promote effectively. Post regularly on your Facebook Page. As well, employ all the regular tactics like promotion on your website, an email blast, promotion on other social media properties, as part of any paid advertising, and in-store signage, etc. Also, consider running a Facebook paid ad campaign to support your promotion as well as listing the promotion on sweepstakes and contest websites.

- Keep the entry form short. The less questions, the higher the conversion rate, so include the necessary fields and no more.

- For contests, make the form of entry as easy as possible. Photos are relatively easy to submit, and babies and pets seem to be the most popular. Videos and essay submissions can also be done, but remember to make it easy. Consider giving a maximum length and sharing examples of submissions to show people how easy it is to enter.

Promotion Applications

Once you have your idea for your sweepstakes or contest, it's time to implement. Again, promotions must be run using "Apps on Facebook." Many companies choose to use an approved third party application provider. These tools are often very easy to use and very affordable, plus you don't have to worry as much about breaking Facebook's terms of use. Here is a list of some of the popular options.

Wildfire
http://www.wildfireapp.com/

Wildfire, recently purchased by Google, is one of the most popular providers. Wildfire's interface is very easy to use and fees are very reasonable. For example, a Standard promotion gets you a custom entry form and branded banner for $25 and $2.99/day. Wildfire promotes to their large base of users to get your promotion going with no additional spend.

Basic	Standard	Premium	White Label
$5 + ¢.99	$25 + $2.99	$250 + $4.99	Call Us
A PROMOTION / PER DAY	A PROMOTION / PER DAY	A PROMOTION / PER DAY	888.274.0929
Unlimited Participants	Unlimited Participants	Unlimited Participants	Unlimited Participants
Any Promotion Type	Any Promotion Type	Any Promotion Type	Any Promotion Type
Standardized Entry Forms	Custom Entry Forms	Custom Entry Forms	Mandatory Likes
No Custom Header Banner	Custom Header Banner	Custom Design	Custom Design
Email Support (48 hours)	Email Support (48 hours)	Email, Chat or Phone	Dedicated Service
TEST DRIVE	TEST DRIVE	TEST DRIVE	CONTACT ME

Offerpop
http://offerpop.com/

Offerpop is another popular, inexpensive, and easy to use application. Campaigns for Pages with less than 100 fans are free.

WOOBOX
http://www.woobox.com

Woobox has several sweepstakes and contest apps that are free or reasonably priced.

NorthSocial
http://northsocial.com/

NorthSocial is also popular and has a variety of applications, including sweepstakes and contest apps.

Strutta
http://www.strutta.com

Strutta offers inexpensive options for small organizations as well as more pricy options that allow for advanced customization, refer a friend incentives, etc.

Some other options to consider are **Fannappz** http://fanappz.com/, **Votigo** http://www.votigo.com/, and **ShortStack** http://www.shortstack.com/.

Since everything Facebook changes so rapidly, start with this list and keep your eyes open for any new options. As you can see, it's relatively easy to run a sweepstakes or contest on Facebook and doing so can be an effective way to achieve business objectives.

ACTION ITEMS

- Watch for current sweepstakes or contests in your News Feed, via email, or on the Facebook Pages of your favorite organizations. Note what you like and don't like.

- Determine if a contest or sweepstakes might make sense for your organization. If so, review the third party application and choose the one that is most appropriate based on capabilities and costs.

- If a contest or sweepstakes is appropriate, set up a test campaign with a great prize, appropriate length of time, and don't forget to promote it.

---

8 Measuring Success

There is no point in being on Facebook if you are not achieving your overall objectives, so it is really important to regularly look at your efforts and achievements. There is so much information available that it is important to look at the right metrics. We like to remember the phrase "What gets measured gets improved upon."

So first, let's look at what data is available. The amount of information and data available can be overwhelming, but it's a good idea to periodically review it and important to focus on the key metrics that will affect how you manage your Facebook Page day to day. Next, let's examine what metrics you might want to focus on and how to view the data.

Tools

There are a number of tools available to view and make sense of your Facebook data. Facebook Insights is Facebook's helpful built in tool. There are a number of third party tools that are also very helpful.

Facebook Insights

The first place to look for Facebook data is Facebook Insights. This is Facebook's own analytics tool and it includes a lot of information, much more than the tools of many other social media properties. Let's dig into what data is available and how to navigate the tool.

You can get to this by clicking on "See all" in the Insights section on any Page that you have Administrator rights, or go to https://www.facebook.com/insights/. On this Page, you will see high-level data for each of your Facebook Pages. To dig deeper, click on "View Insights."

Facebook Insights has four tabs—Overview, Likes, Reach, and Talking About This. The Overview tab includes important information including total Likes, People Talking About This, Weekly Total Reach, and information for individual posts. Likes is at the top left and is self explanatory. A drawback of Facebook Insights is that only the current number of Likes is available. In order to get the number of Likes on a particular day, it is necessary to use a third party analytics tool.

People Talking About This is also an important metric. This counts all activity on a Page—new Likes, posts to your Wall, Likes/Comments or Shares to a post, answers a Question posted, responses to an Event, mentions of the Page, tags of the Page in a photo, and checks-in at a place or recommends of a place. This is a good gauge as to whether overall activity is up or down. Note that if there is an ad campaign in progress, this number can be skewed up.

Weekly total reach is the number of unique people that have seen a Page's content. This will also be skewed high if there is an ad campaign in progress.

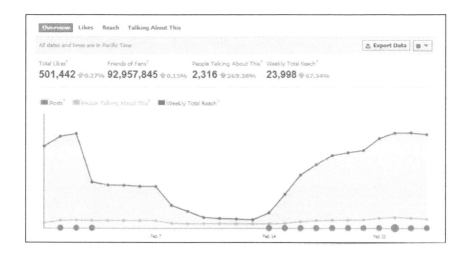

At the bottom of the Overview tab is a list of the most recent Page Posts. Click on Older Posts to see more. Facebook will show you a maximum of about thirty posts. This is a great way to see how individual Posts performed. Each Post includes the date it was published, the Post copy (click to see the Post), Reach, Engaged Users, Talking About This, and Virality.

TIP: Look at your recent posts and see which did the best in terms of Reach, Engaged Users, Talking About This, and Virality. Use this information to improve future posts.

Reach measures the number of unique people that saw a post. It is interesting to see how this varies from post to post. You will see that Facebook favors some posts. For example, posts with images are often favored, as well as Questions. Posts that mention a holiday or limited time offer are often favored. If your posts have been doing well in terms of engagement, then new posts will be served to more people. This goes back to EdgeRank, which we talked about earlier. Finally, this number includes reach to all friends of those that Like, Share, or Comment. So, the higher the engagement on an individual post, the higher the reach.

Engaged Users is the number of unique people that have interacted with a post. This includes Likes, Comments, Shares, answering a Question, clicks on photos, and any other clicks. Click on each number to see interaction by type. Helpful hint—you are able to see the number of people who gave negative feedback, which includes hiding a post or reporting as spam. This data can be exported for deeper analysis.

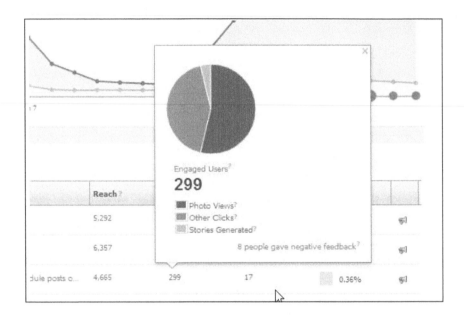

The Talking About This column is the number of unique people who have Liked, Commented, or Shared a post, answered a question, or responded to an event. Click on the number to see the breakout.

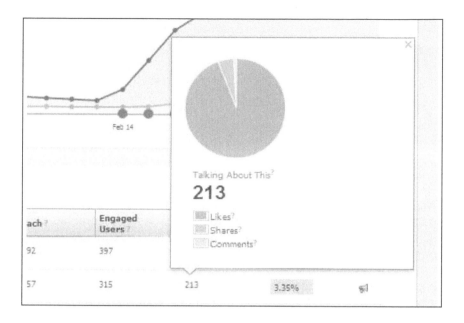

Virality is the number of people that have Liked, Commented, or Shared a post divided by the reach. Look at how your posts do in terms of reach, overall engagement, and virality, and keep improving your posts (timing, type, content, etc.) based on this.

The Likes tab includes interesting information about the people that have Liked a Page. This includes demographic information such as gender and age, and geographic data including countries, cities, and languages. Lastly, the tab includes data on Like sources. This lets you know if people are Liking from the Facebook web Page, via mobile, etc. This information can be sorted by date, and data can be exported.

TIP: Look for any spikes in new Likes or Unlikes and see what you posted on that day in order to mimic and increase Likes, or stop doing in the case of a large number of Unlikes.

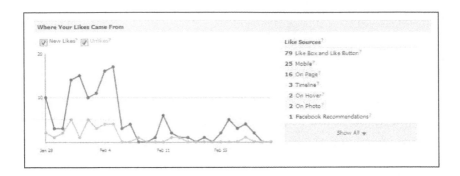

The next tab is the Reach tab. This dives into who was reached by posts and any Facebook ads. Facebook provides demographic data including gender and age, and geographic data including cities and countries of the users that were reached, as well as languages.

Next, Facebook provides information about how people were reached. Facebook breaks out by organic (people that have Liked a Page and see posts), viral (people that are friends of people that engage with a post), or paid (people that see a Facebook paid ad). This is really interesting data that shows you how virality can greatly increase the reach of a post.

Facebook also breaks out users by frequency. This is interesting information. If the majority of your users are only seeing your posts once during a period, then you may want to increase posts. If frequency seems high, you may want to decrease the number of posts.

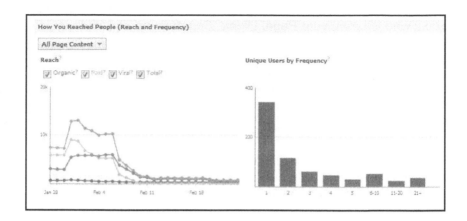

Lastly, you can see information about visits to your Facebook Page including all page views, unique visitors, views by tab, and external referrers. Data from this tab can also be exported for deeper analysis.

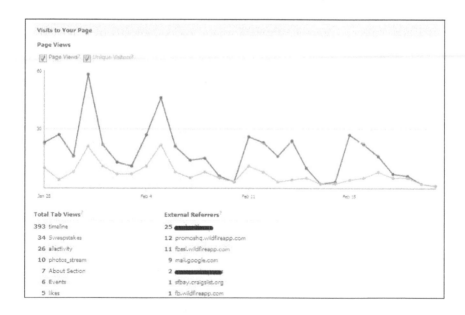

The last tab is called Talking About This and dives into information about who is Liking your Page, Liking, Commenting and Sharing your posts, answering Questions and responding to Events, mentioning the Page, as well as posts by others. By looking at the gender and age data, you can see who is engaging with your Page, and tweak the Page and posts to better meet the needs of the audience, or revise if this is not your target audience.

TIP: The most engaged users are often your biggest fans and brand advocates. Learn about them to create content that they will like as well as how to converse with them.

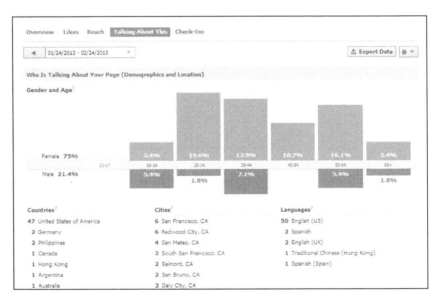

So, as you can see there is a lot of helpful data available in Facebook Insights. Of course, the platform will continue to evolve so use this guide as a starting point and look out for any new data that becomes available.

Bit.ly

Another helpful measurement tool is bit.ly https://bitly.com/. Bit.ly is a url shortener. Here, you can track clicks on links (to your website, your blog articles, or third party articles). This lets you know which types of content is resonating with your Facebook audience.

TIME	sort by Clicks on Your Link ⌄	CLICKS VIA YOUR SHORTLINK Past 7 days	Total	TOTAL CLICKS	TOTAL SAVES
Jul 16 2011	How To Turn Off Facebook Chat or Edit ...		32	71	4
Jan 17 2012	3 Successful Google+ Pages and Why The...		14	212	30
Feb 24 2011	http://rachelmelia.com/2011/02/24/ho...		9	9	1
Feb 24 2011	How To Measure Your Social Media Eff...		8	8	2
Jul 27 2011	www.facebook.com/business		8	1490	93
Jul 21 2011	10 Ways To Increase Your Facebook Likes		8	26	4
May 27 2011	New Social Media Research: This Week i...		7	47	9
May 11 2011	How to Build a Free Social Media Monit...		7	147	8
Nov 20	www.socialmediaexaminer.com/integr...		6	118	36
May 28	5 Simple Metrics to Track Your Social M...		6	262	36

Bit.ly also shows clicks by day, referrers, and locations of clicks. Clicks by day can give an indication of which days of the week are best for you to post content. Referrers is interesting as it shows if clicks are on Facebook, Facebook mobile, via email clients, etc.

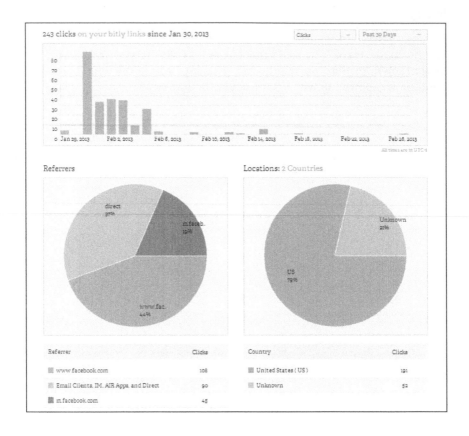

TIP: bit.ly is a handy tool to see which links resonate with your audience and when they are clicking.

Google Analytics

Google Analytics is a very helpful (and free) analytics tool. Google Analytics allows you to track traffic from Facebook as well as all other sources. It also allows you to see pages per visit, visit length, how many of the visitors are new, and the bounce rate. You can also see how many visits are from the Facebook website vs. mobile. This allows you to see how Facebook is performing in terms of driving traffic to a website or blog versus other sources. The data can easily be pulled by date.

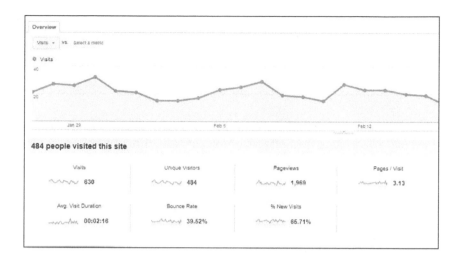

Even better, by setting up Goals, Google Analytics can tell you how many website conversions or sales came from Facebook. You can also set up campaigns to gauge success from various Facebook efforts.

Google Analytics now has a Social section in the interface. Here, you can see referrals, which Pages social visitors landed on, conversions broken out by last interaction and assisted conversions, data from any social plugins, and the social visitor flow. Google Analytics is a highly valuable free tool in your marketing arsenal.

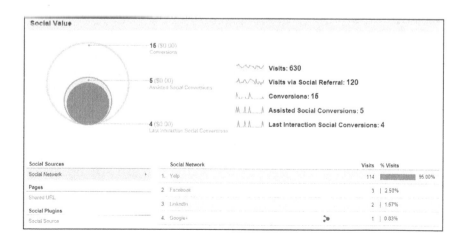

Beyond those very helpful free tools, there are many other tools that can help you gauge the effectiveness of your Facebook marketing efforts. Here are some to try.

There are several social media management tools that include measurement components. Two good tools are HootSuite and Sprout Social.

HootSuite

HootSuite integrates with Facebook Insights so that data is available via the HootSuite dashboard. HootSuite also allows you to track clicks and mentions. A powerful component of HootSuite is that it integrates with Google Analytics so you can track conversions and campaign performance. Lastly, HootSuite has customizable reports. Free accounts include the ability to track clicks and mentions, as well as basic reports. Paid accounts start at $9.99/month and include Facebook Insights and Google Analytics integration as well as an enhanced Analytics report.

Sprout Social

Sprout Social is another social media management tool that includes a measurement component. Sprout Social starts at $39/month. The starting price includes Facebook integration, brand monitoring, and reports and analytics. The next version up, at $59/month includes Google Analytics integration. Sprout Social has a very visual interface, which some people like. The interface also includes helpful information like reach and engagement. Sprout Social consolidates the most interesting information from Facebook Insights and Google Analytics onto a colorful report, which can be easily exported to a PDF document for sharing. The drawback is that this report is not customizable.

		AVG. PER POST	TOTAL
■ Photo 52	Reach	371	21.9k
■ Link 6			
■ Status 4	People Talking About This	14	814
	Engagement	11%	8%

CONTENT BREAKDOWN A breakdown of how your individual posts performed

Message Sent ▾	Reach	Engaged	Talking	Likes	Comments	Shares	Engagement
February 22, 2013 at 8:30 am	188	24	15	15	–	1	12.77%
February 21, 2013 at 8:40 am	70	9	4	4	–	–	12.86%
February 20, 2013 at 2:40 pm	75	3	1	–	–	1	4%

For more Facebook analysis, there are several good tools, and more debuting all the time. Here are a few:

SocialDon http://www.socialdon.com/
Free. Allows you to compare data between Facebook Pages.

Quintly http://www.quintly.com/
Free to $399/month. Comprehensive and in-depth analytics.

Pagelever http://Pagelever.com/
$99/month to $599/month. Has over 200 graphs and metrics not found on Facebook Insights. A very robust tool to analyze posts and fans.

Blitzmetrics https://blitzmetrics.com/
$500/month. Competitive benchmarking, geographic mapping of fans, fan demographics, and more.

For enterprise sized organizations with larger budgets, here are some leaders.

Adobe Social http://www.adobe.com/products/social.html
Contact sales department for pricing. A very powerful tool that integrates with Omniture to provide data through conversion.

Salesforce Marketing Cloud (formerly Radian6 and BuddyMedia)
http://www.salesforce.com/socialmarketing/
Contact sales department for pricing. Includes monitoring, listening, social media management, and insights.

All this data is great and can be very useful for understanding and improving your efforts, but it can also be overwhelming. At the end of the day, it's important to track several key high level metrics that usually include data from various sources such as site referrals, leads, or conversions.

Large organizations, or those with bigger budgets, can use solutions like Adobe Social or Salesforce Marketing Cloud. There is currently no great solution for small and mid-size organizations. HootSuite and Sprout Social come close. As mentioned before, HootSuite integrates with Google Analytics, but, it is not easy to create a nice customized report. Sprout Social also integrates with Google Analytics, and the report is nice, but it is not possible to customize the report or integrate conversion information. These leaders will likely improve their dashboards in the future.

Many small and mid-size organizations create a simple Excel reporting dashboard to track important metrics and progress meeting business objectives.

Creating A Reporting Dashboard

The reporting dashboard may contain information on Facebook growth including Page Likes and Unlikes, as well as reach, engagement rate, and performance against overall objectives. It might also incorporate important metrics including traffic to your blog or website, audience engagement, mentions, improved brand sentiment, leads, reduction in customer service calls, and revenue.

Here is a simple reporting dashboard that can be tweaked for your business' unique objectives and reporting capabilities. You can add other social media properties to the dashboard to compare high level performance.

	January	% Increase	February	% Increase
Facebook				
Total Likes				
New Likes				
Unlikes				
Reach per post				
Total reach				
Interaction rate				
Referals to website				
Email opt-ins				
Sales				
Revenue				

As you can see, there is no shortage of data and tools, and the data and tools are certain to evolve over time. So, choose the tools that are most helpful to you, measure your efforts, and continually improve your Facebook success.

ACTION ITEMS

- Go to Facebook Insights https://www.facebook.com/insights/ and see the wealth of information available there.

- If you have Google Analytics set up for your website, explore the information available there, especially Referrals and Social. If not set up already, consider setting up Conversion Goals.

- Create a reporting dashboard.

- If it makes sense for your organization to utilize a more sophisticated tool, check out the ones mentioned.

---

9 Facebook Applications For Pages

Facebook makes it very easy to create a nice looking Page with Timeline. If you want to customize your Page by adding tabs, there are many third party applications available. There are individual applications for Pages as well as suites. It is also possible to create your own application.

First, you may be wondering what an application is and why you would want one. Applications generally reside on a tab that can be accessed from a tab image on a Page's Timeline. Some examples of applications are those that support sweepstakes and contests, as we discussed before, as well as applications for social media properties like YouTube and Pinterest, applications for email services like Constant Contact and MailChimp, applications for e-commerce functionality, etc.

As with your other Facebook initiatives, use of Facebook applications should map back to your overall objectives such as site referrals, increasing size of email list, increasing brand affinity, etc.

Links to
application
tabs →

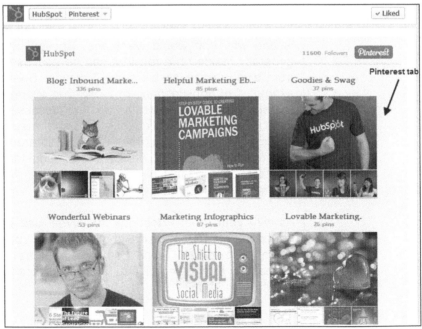

It used to be easy to search for applications within Facebook's application directory https://www.facebook.com/appcenter/. You could search for an application, for example Twitter, and a list of relevant applications would come up with number of users and ratings. Now, this directory is much more consumer focused, and there is no search functionality.

A helpful third party website that lists Facebook Page applications is appbistro http://appbistro.com/. It lists many individual applications and suites of applications and includes reviews and costs, if any. This is a good place to look for relevant applications, but note it is not comprehensive.

As a starting point, here is a list of some popular applications by category. As with all things Facebook, new applications are released all the time. It is best to double-check that there is not a new better option available.

Social Media Applications

Adding tabs for your various social media properties can be a good way to pique people's interest and hopefully get them to click through and engage with you outside Facebook. Many of these are free (or the providers offer one or two applications free). Here are some top application providers for social media properties.

Twitter

Involver http://www.involver.com/applications/
WOOBOX http://www.woobox.com/twitter

YouTube

Involver http://www.involver.com/applications/
North Social http://northsocial.com/apps/video-channel/

Pinterest

WOOBOX http://www.woobox.com/pinterest
Tabsite http://www.tabsite.com/engagementapps

Instagram

North Social http://northsocial.com/apps/instagram/

Tabsite

http://www.tabsite.com/engagementapps

Blog

Involver http://www.involver.com/applications/
Tabsite http://www.tabsite.com/engagementapps

Flickr

Involver http://www.involver.com/applications/

Email Applications

Most email providers have their own applications to create Facebook tabs with email opt-in forms. There is no cost with your existing subscription. It is easy to add this functionality and a great way to allow Facebook fans to opt-in to your email database.

Constant Contact http://www.constantcontact.com/index.jsp

MailChimp http://mailchimp.com/

Vertical Response http://www.verticalresponse.com/

TIP: It is a great idea to add an email sign up tab. This allows any fan that wants to sign up for emails from you to do so.

Other Popular Tools

There are applications to create tabs for many popular tools. Here are two.

Eventbrite

Eventbrite for Facebook Pages http://eventbistro.com/

SurveyMonkey

SurveyMonkey
http://blog.surveymonkey.com/blog/2011/09/12/facebook-survey/

Promotions

We talked about sweepstakes and contests earlier. Here are several popular promotions applications.

Wildfire http://www.wildfireapp.com/

NorthSocial http://northsocial.com/

Offerpop http://offerpop.com/

WOOBOX http://www.woobox.com

Strutta http://www.strutta.com

Fannappz http://fanappz.com/

Votigo http://www.votigo.com/

ShortStack http://www.shortstack.com/

TIP: Remember when you create your sweepstakes or contest using a third party application to customize the thumbnail image. This will make the tab more noticeable and match your look and feel.

E-commerce

Payvment http://www.payvment.com/

While e-commerce hasn't taken off on Facebook like some thought it might, you may still want to consider adding the functionality. Payvment is the leader in the space.

Original Tabs

There are applications that allow you to create your own original tabs. Here are a few leaders.

North Social iframe editor
http://northsocial.com/apps/iframe-editor/

Involver Static HTML http://www.involver.com/applications/

Lujure https://lujure.com/
Lujure allows you to create original tabs using drag and drop.

GroSocial http://www.grosocial.com/
GroSocial allows you to create original tabs using drag and drop.

Suites Of Applications

There are several companies that have suites of Facebook applications. Often, they offer one or more applications for free and require a fee to gain access to more. Here is a list.

North Social http://northsocial.com/
North Social has over 18 applications including Instagram, an iframe editor, sweepstakes, deals, videos, and more. Costs range from $0.99/day to $8.99/day.

Involver http://www.involver.com/applications/

Two apps are free. Contact Involver for costs for more apps. Involver has apps for RSS feed, Twitter, YouTube, Flickr, Static HTML, photos, customer service, Scribd, forms, polls, Klout Coupons, etc.

Tabsite http://www.tabsite.com/engagementapps

Two tabs are free. Fees range from $10/month to $25/month. Tabsite has apps for deals (group, share, Pinterest), Pinterest, Instagram, social review, photo gallery, contest/sweepstakes, products for sale, RSS, YouTube, email, etc.

Pagemodo http://www.Pagemodo.com/

One tab is free. Fees range from $6.25/month to $33.25/month. Functionality includes the ability to add tabs for videos, contact forms, maps and locations, coupons, Twitter, newsletter (Aweber, MailChimp, or Constant Contact), products, custom HTMl, and more. Pagemodo offers the ability to include fangates before any content.

Lujure https://lujure.com/

One tab is free. Prices range from $30/month to $300/month. Customizable tabs. Include content such as YouTube videos, RSS feeds, live video (from Vpype), slideshows, flash, chat, and more.

GroSocial http://www.grosocial.com/

$19.95 to $49.95. Customizable tabs. Includes content such as sweep-stakes and contests, lead capture forms, coupons, and social media properties. Includes Twitter customization and analytics.

Create Your Own

If you are a developer or have access to a developer, you may want to create your own application. Here is the link to do that. https://developers.facebook.com/docs/guides/canvas/

As you can see, there are many free and paid applications available for adding new tabs to your Facebook Page. Before you spend too much time and money on these, keep in mind that the majority of activity happens on the News Feed versus on the Facebook Page. Free applications might make the most sense for many organizations. For larger organizations, or to achieve priority business objectives, a cost might be justified. As always, keep your eyes open for new and better tools that come out frequently in this fast changing space.

ACTION ITEMS

- Visit the Timelines of some of your favorite Facebook Pages and look at their applications. See how they are accessed via the application tab thumbnail under the Cover Image.

- Install a few free applications—a couple that are easy to install and appropriate for many organizations include an email opt-in form and tabs for social media properties, Pinterest is particularly popular now.

- Consider using an application to create your own customized tabs.

- Consider suites of applications if warranted by your Facebook objectives and budget.

---

10 Facebook Plugins

Facebook Plugins are widgets that bring Facebook functionality to your site. Facebook currently has 11 plugins, but is about to eliminate one, leaving 10 plugins at your disposal. They can be accessed from the Facebook site http://bit.ly/gHEA54.[1] It is easy to configure these and grab the code, and you can implement many of them yourself if you are a bit technical, or have a developer do it.

Here is a rundown of the various plugins.

Like Button

The Like Button is probably the most popular Facebook plugin and you have likely seen it on many sites. It can be placed next to any content on a website and allows people to easily share to their Facebook profile. It is very common to see Like Buttons next to blog articles. The Like Button is often also placed next to content on other website pages including the home page, product pages, etc. You can also use the Like Button as a way for website visitors to Like your Facebook Page.

---

1. https://developers.facebook.com/docs/plugins/

If you are going to implement only one or two plugins, this one should be seriously considered. It is easy to implement and a great way to get people to share your content with the Facebook friends as well as Like your Facebook Page.

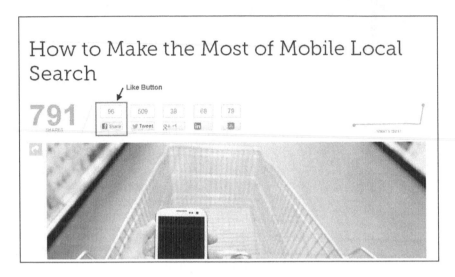

It is easy to customize the plugin and create the code. Facebook allows you to select whether or not to include a Send button next to the Like button. A Send Button allows users to send content to a friend or group on Facebook or via email. You can select the layout—either the Standard layout which is a horizontal button, Button Count which is the horizontal button with the number of Likes, or the Box Count which has the horizontal button with the number of Likes in a box above the button. You can also select the width of the plugin, whether or not to show people's Facebook profile pictures below the button, the verb to display—Like or Recommend, colors and the font.

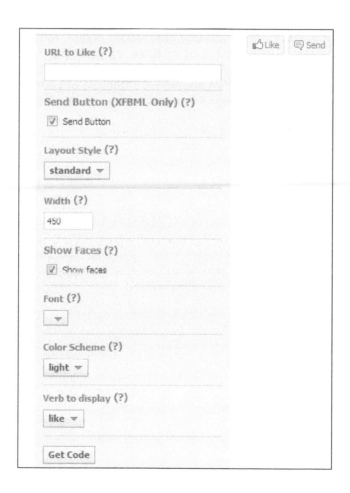

TIP: Install the Like button next to shareable content like blog posts, etc. For more Facebook Page Likes, consider installing it on your website as a way for users to Like the Page without leaving your website.

Like Box

The Like Box is also a very common Facebook plugin. It allows users to like your Facebook Page without leaving your website. It is very often installed on blogs as well as other web pages including home pages, About Us, Contact Us, and Newsroom pages, etc. This plugin uses social proof in the form of pictures of your friends that have already Liked a Facebook Page to make a person more likely to click Like. This is also a plugin that should be at the top of your plugin consideration list as it is a way to easily increase the number of your Facebook followers.

The Like Box can be easily customized. Facebook allows you to change the width and height, color scheme, and border, decide whether or not to show faces of fans, whether or not to show a stream of your Facebook Page activity, and determine whether or not to show a header at the top of the Like Box. It is more common to show faces and not Facebook Page activity.

TIP: Most organizations show faces as social proof, but don't show the stream of posts.

Comments

The Comments plugin is another plugin that is fairly easy to implement. It allows a person to comment on a website and easily share the comment to their Facebook profile. This is commonly used following blog articles and can also be used on any other pages where people might like to comment, for example product pages, etc. When a person shares a comment to their Facebook profile, their friends can also comment on that in their Facebook feed or in the Comments box on the website. The thread stays intact on Facebook as well as the site where the comment originated. Facebook allows some customization of this plugin.

Several of the plugins require a bit more technical expertise. The Activity Feed, Recommendations Bar, and Recommendations Box plugins must include Open Graph Markup so that Facebook can pull content from your website. The Registration and Login Button plugins require site platforms that support the plugins and significant effort by IT teams.

Recommendations Bar

The Recommendations Bar plugin is most often used on blogs and news sites. It shows up on the bottom right (or left) side of a website page as a collapsed box and enlarges after a certain amount of time. It stays fixed next to a person's browser as they scroll up and down a page. The plugin allows a user to Like the Facebook Page as well as provides recommendations for other content, usually articles, on the site. This is a little trickier to implement as you must include Open Graph Markup on your articles so Facebook knows how to display them.

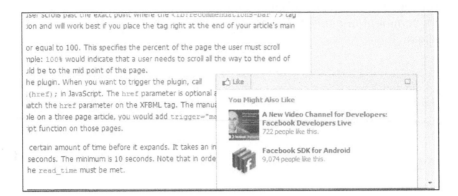

Recommendations Box

The Recommendations Box displays personalized recommendations of your content to site visitors. Facebook sources this content based on social interactions with urls on your site. If a Facebook user is logged into your site, the plugin will give preference to content friends have interacted with.

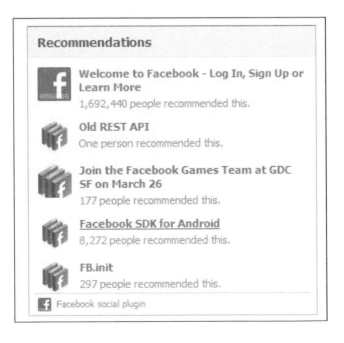

Registration

The Registration plugin allows a person to register for a website using their Facebook registration information. If a user is logged in, fields are automatically populated. This can lower the barrier of entry to register for a website, therefore increasing the number of registered users. Another benefit is that when a person registers using their Facebook login, their Facebook information is passed over to the site providing much more valuable data about the new users' demographic information as well as Likes and interests.

Note that Facebook's Registration plugin does not have to be the only mechanism to register for a site. The Registration button can be used alongside a standard registration form. The Registration plugin requires IT help and additional effort to implement.

Login Button

The Login button allows a person to login to a website using their Facebook profile. This can make it easier, and therefore more likely that a person will login to your website. By getting a person to login using Facebook, you gain access to valuable demographic and interest data. This requires IT help and some effort, but is worthwhile for many sites. The Login Button is highly used across the web.

Other Facebook plugins include the Send Button, Subscribe Button, and Facepile. The Send Button can be a part of the Like Button or used separately. It allows users to send content to Facebook friends or Groups as well as via email. It is somewhat less used than the Like button. The Subscribe Button allows people to subscribe to Facebook users from a website. Sometimes this is used on About Us Pages, on employee information Pages, etc. The Facepile plugin displays thumbnail images of Facebook users that have taken an action on your website including liking a particular piece of content or registering for the site, etc.

Facebook plugins are great for multiple objectives including increasing the reach of your content, increasing Facebook Page Likes, and making it easier for site visitors to login while gaining valuable data. Choose to implement the ones that make sense for your organization.

TIP: If your organization has the resources, add the Registration and Login buttons for easier site registration/login as well as a way to gain access to Facebook's data on your website visitors.

ACTION ITEMS

- Install the easy-to-install and highly valuable plugins on your website/blog—Consider the Like button and the Like Box.

- Consider other plugins like Comments, Recommendations, etc.

- If you have the resources, consider the more labor intensive to install plugins including the Registration and Login Buttons.

11 Frequently Asked Questions

We have answered many frequently asked questions in detail throughout the book. Short answers to some of these questions as well as answers to additional questions follow.

Should I create a Facebook Page for my business? It depends! If you are a business that relies on many customers and wants to keep in touch with your customers, a Facebook Page might make sense. While it is free to set up a Facebook Page, it will require time and effort to maintain it. Make sure your Page meets business objectives.

How do I set up a Facebook Page? For detailed instructions see Chapter 2, Getting Started. Here is the link to set up your Page.
https://www.facebook.com/pages/create.php

How do I claim my Facebook username? Facebook will ask you to do this when setting up your Page. If you have an existing Page and no username, go to
https://www.facebook.com/username/

How do I change my Facebook Page name? If you have less than 100 fans, you can change your Page name in your Page Settings. Once you hit that limit, you're out of luck. The only way around that is if you have a large ad spend, or contract an agency (Jesse Stay can also do this for you on a consulting basis with his relationships at Facebook).

How often should I post? That really depends on your resources, objectives, and audience. There has been a lot of research on the optimal posting frequency (see Chapter 3 Developing Engaging Content for more details). What it often comes down to is your resources (how much time can you spend producing content and managing the Page), objectives (an objective of driving significant traffic to your blog might require a high number of posts, etc.), and audience (some audiences want to hear from organizations more than others). A general rule of thumb used to be one post/day. Many now consider that low since posts with Timeline now reach a lower percentage of total fans.

How many posts are too many? Again, this is tough to answer. News outlets can do multiple daily posts. For other types of organizations, two or three posts are probably on the high end as you don't want to annoy your audience. Make sure it is good content that people like receiving. Check Insights to see how number of posts correlates to Unlikes.

What should I post? Content your audience finds helpful and interesting. Ideally this should be original content, and make it as image rich as possible. Also make sure that it is relevant and maps back to your business objectives.

How can I tell if I am doing well? Visit Facebook Insights for helpful analytics (see Chapter 8 Measuring Success for a full explanation). In particular, look at your Engagement to see which posts are getting interaction. Beyond engagement, make sure to track how you are meeting your objectives such as traffic to your website, sales, reach, reduced customer service calls, and more.

How can I increase post engagement? See Chapter 3 for details. Here are some quick tips. Post at times when your audience is online, post images whenever possible, make your copy short, and include a call to action.

How can I increase Likes? There are lots of ways to increase Likes. First, put links everywhere—on your website, on other social media properties, on email signatures, on signage, as well as promote via other social media, on any paid advertising, etc. You can also put the Facebook Like box and other plugins on your website and blog. Beyond that, many organizations do paid advertising and promotions to increase fans.

Is it hard to advertise on Facebook? Yes and no. Facebook has a do-it-yourself solution that is relatively easy to figure out. For best results, you want to do some testing of different ad types as well as various targets, copy, images, etc. This can be a little daunting. See Chapter 6 Advertising on Facebook for more details. Here is the link to set up an ad buy **https://www.facebook.com/ads**. Promoted Posts are very easy to implement and Sponsored Stories are fairly easy to implement.

What are some objectives that can be achieved on Facebook? You can achieve many objectives. Some common objectives are staying top of mind, letting fans know about coupons and discounts, increasing awareness and affinity, driving traffic to a website or blog, collecting email addresses, selling product, gaining product feedback, and lowering customer service costs.

What are Facebook plugins? Facebook Plugins are widgets that can be added to your website to extend Facebook's functionality to your site. Facebook currently has 10 plugins you can use. Some of the more popular ones include the Like Button, Like Box, Comments Box, Registration, and Login Button.

12 Additional Resources

There are many great sources of helpful Facebook content. Here are some of our favorites.

Social Media Examiner—A social media blog with lots of great Facebook content. Social Media Examiner hosts an online conference, The Facebook Success Summit, once a year. The Summit features many of the top Facebook experts and takes place over a several week period.
http://www.socialmediaexaminer.com/

All Facebook—A website dedicated to all things Facebook. Often breaks Facebook news and produces a lot of very helpful content.
http://allfacebook.com/

Inside Facebook—Another website that focuses on everything Facebook. It is a great source for Facebook news.
http://www.insidefacebook.com/

Mari Smith—Dubbed the Pied Piper of Facebook, Mari shares the latest and greatest new features and how-tos with her large following. http://www.marismith.com/

Mashable—A well-regarded technology blog that publishes many articles about Facebook. http://mashable.com/

Hubspot—A marketing software company that produces a very good blog with a lot of Facebook content. http://blog.hubspot.com/

I'm on Facebook—Now What??? **Facebook Page**—The Facebook Page that accompanies this book.
https://www.facebook.com/fbbook

For Facebook content from the writers of this book, visit the following blogs:
Jesse Stay—http://www.jessestay.com/
Jason Alba—http://jasonalba.com/
Rachel Melia—http://rachelmelia.com

13 Conclusion And The Future Of Facebook Marketing

Facebook took the internet by storm and brought social media to the masses. There are now 1 billion people using the site monthly, from all around the world. Mark Zuckerberg has said that Facebook was built to accomplish a social mission—to make the world more open and connected, and he is well on his way to doing that.

Facebook, along with other popular social media properties, has revolutionized marketing. Where marketing was once dominated by one way messages to the masses, it is now much more relationship based. While marketing used to require big budgets and favor large organizations, it can now be done much less expensively, leveling the playing field for organizations of all sizes as well as organizations from different geographic regions. It is an exciting time to be a business owner or be in marketing.

Look for more exciting changes in the months and years ahead. While user growth is slowing in countries like the United States and Europe, where we are close to saturation, expect more growth in Asia and developing countries. Facebook is facilitating this growth by making it easier for organizations to reach a global audience. Facebook has just announced Global Pages, which allow brands to maintain a single fan Page with localized experiences for users in different countries. Also expect growth beyond the desktop as more people move to smart phones and tablets. With mobile growth, look for product updates and new and improved ways to market to the non-desktop audience. Search is also an area to expect major changes and improvements given the data available to work with and desire to monetize.

We're passionate about the current and future marketing opportunities on Facebook. Good luck in your Facebook marketing efforts!

Afterword By Michael Stelzner

Facebook has changed marketing in the same way television did when it was first introduced. Yes, we've always had ways to connect with people via email, forums, and blogs. But Facebook changed everything.

All of a sudden, marketing became personal again.

Just like the intimate experience of gathering around the television in days past to enjoy a show as a family, Facebook provides friends and family a way to "connect" while miles apart and with little effort.

It is for this precise reason that Facebook has radically changed marketing.

Now people can have very intimate experiences with their friends and family, alongside the brands and businesses they love.

Because Facebook is ubiquitous, it provides an incredible opportunity for marketers to build a community, solicit feedback on new products, service customers, and much more.

At Social Media Examiner, we've seen more than 100,000 fans come together, support one another, and so much more. It has literally changed our business for the better.

Facebook isn't going anywhere. Smart businesses will figure out how to leverage its power and grow their business. Those that ignore it will turn aside from a large group of their prospective customers.

What will you do?

—Michael Stelzner

About The Authors

Jason Alba is the CEO and creator of JibberJobber.com, a web-based system to organize and manage a job search (and the networking you do between job searches). Jason is a certified Personal Branding Strategist and popular blogger and speaker about career management and social tools for professionals. Jason wrote *I'm on LinkedIn—Now What???*, one of the first books on using LinkedIn. He also wrote *I'm on Facebook—Now What???* and is finishing two more books (*Eight Lunches*, for entrepreneurs and a book on social media etiquette). Jason maintains several blogs including JibberJobber.com/blog, and contributes to the AOL Jobs blog. In his spare time he created the LinkedIn for Job Seekers DVD. Jason has an IT and business background and earned a Computer Information Systems degree and an MBA.

Jesse Stay is a speaker, author, blogger, and entrepreneur, who writes and consults on the topics of social media and new media architecture, bridging the gap between "technical" and "social" for both marketers and developers. Jesse has written four books—his latest two, *Facebook Application Development For Dummies* http://stay.am/dummiesbook, and the recently released *Google+ For Dummies* http://stay.am/gplusdummies show the breadth of knowledge Jesse has to offer. Jesse was also named one of 20 developers to follow on Twitter http://mashable.com/2009/06/04/developers-tips-twitter/ and one of 10 entrepreneurs to follow on Twitter http://mashable.com/2009/10/29/entrepreneurs-twitter-follow/ by the top Tech blog Mashable.com http://mashable.com/.

His unique technology background has enabled him to help others understand the new mesh of technology, marketing, PR, and customer service, which social media has come to be, and how they can deeply integrate these technologies into their own environments. Jesse has consulted for top 10 Facebook applications, large corporations, social media applications with millions of users, and has helped many people become successful through their social media efforts to merge technology with marketing. Jesse has built his own profitable social media applications in the hundreds of thousands of users. In addition to building and consulting for top social media applications, Jesse has been successful in managing Social Media campaigns for Facebook

Pages in the hundreds of thousands of fans to even millions, some of them his own Facebook Pages. During his day job, Jesse serves as a Social Media Strategist for The Church of Jesus Christ of Latter-day Saints http://mormon.org/, an organization with over 14 million members, some of the largest humanitarian and service efforts in the world, and a very unique international strategy for social media. (Yes, he's a Mormon http://mormon.org/me/1H2Y-eng/)

Jesse also hosts his own successful blog, Stay N Alive http://staynalive.com/, perhaps the #1 tech blog in Utah and is regularly featured on Techmeme.com http://techmeme.com/. Aside from that, Jesse's articles have been featured on sites such as LouisGray.com http://louisgray.com/, the top two Facebook blogs, InsideFacebook http://insidefacebook.com/ and AllFacebook http://allfacebook.com/, as well as Venturebeat http://venturebeat.com/. You can also see the coverage and breadth of Jesse's influence on Delicious http://delicious.com/jessestay/coverage. You can find him on his blog http://staynalive.com/, on Google+ http://profiles.google.com/jessestay, on Facebook http://facebook.com/stay, or on LinkedIn http://www.linkedin.com/in/facebook.

Book him for your next speaking engagement!

Rachel Melia is an Online Marketing Consultant specializing in Facebook marketing. Rachel enjoys helping clients build vibrant social media communities that achieve their business objectives.

Rachel's background includes many years at San Francisco advertising agencies on well-known clients including Kodak Gallery, Microsoft, Palm, Siebel, and Tivo.

Rachel became a consultant seven years ago and has worked with start-ups and small and medium-sized businesses as well as non-profits and government organizations across categories including health, travel, parenting, personal finance, food and beverage, technology, and mobile.

Along with working closely with ongoing clients, Rachel regularly speaks about social media and Facebook marketing.

Rachel is based in Silicon Valley where she was born and raised. She has a Bachelors in Communication from Santa Clara University.

Read Rachel's blog at http://www.rachelmelia.com and contact Rachel at http://www.linkedin.com/in/rachelmelia/.

Other Happy About® Books

Purchase these books at Happy About http://happyabout.com or at other online and physical bookstores.

I'm on LinkedIn—Now What??? (3rd Edition)

This new edition focuses on strategies and tactics to help you understand what LinkedIn is and how it fits into your online marketing strategy (whether it is a personal marketing strategy or a business/corporate marketing strategy).

Paperback: $19.95
eBook: $14.95

Storytelling about Your Brand Online & Offline

Using this book, professionals and executives of all types, entrepreneurs, consultants, musicians, academics and students will undergo a "personal branding process."

Paperback: $22.95
eBook: $16.95

#GOOGLE+ for BUSINESS
tweet Book01

Starting with tips on creating a compelling profile, Janet explains hangouts, circles, and more before tying it all together with proven techniques for developing a coherent Google+ strategy.

Paperback: $19.95
eBook: $14.95

Social Media Success!

This book is a launch pad for successful social media engagement. It shows how to identify the right networks, find the influencers, the people you want to talk to and which tools will work the best for you.

Paperback: $19.95
eBook: $14.95